Beauty – Power – Divinity in Motion

Phantoms of Faith Series

Volume II

E. D. Allen

APOTHEOSIS

Denver, Colorado

Apotheosis, LLC
P.O. Box 102996
Denver, Colorado 80250

Phone: 800 704-8724

www.apotheosisonc.com
info@apotheosisone.com

Printed in the United States of America
First Edition 2020

The publisher and author are not responsible for websites (or their content) that arc not owned or operated by either of them.

Publisher's Note: Locales and public names are sometimes used for atmospheric purposes. Any resemblance to actual people, living or dead, or to businesses, companies, events, institutions, or locales is completely coincidental.

Bible quotations and references (unless noted otherwise) are from the New American Standard Bible produced by the LOCKMAN FOUNDATION.

Book Cover Photo: Mariah Ehlert Photography Denver, Colorado
Cover Design: Apotheosis

Library of Congress Cataloging-in-Publication Data

Allen, Ellis D.

WOMAN: Beauty - Power - Divinity in Motion

Phantoms of Faith Series: Volume 2

ISBN: 978-0-578-94217-9

Preface to Series

The premise for the Phantom of Faith Series is twofold. First, I am under the conviction that those serving or have knowledge in sacred texts, religion, social sciences, and medicine should chronicle their experience in these disciplines, especially where the tenets of these intersect with the public square. Second, the realization that one of the many challenges facing the 21st century Church is remaining relevant to a progressive world, while trying not to corrupt God's word while fulfilling her appointed mandate.

Fearing antiquity, she chases reformation. Progress and reformation do not always equate to maturity. I do not mean reformation in the traditional theological sense, but the perpetual restructuring of the church in its futile attempt to appear relevant, appease its membership and remain competitive with the secular world. In her efforts to garner legitimacy as an institution that speaks for God and that seeks the good of humanity, segments of the faith community have developed spiritual cognitive distortions, inadvertently presenting the church as a group of people immature, weak-minded and delusional.

Cognitive distortion is a clinical term that describes a faulty thought process where one holds certain ideas or beliefs contrary to normalcy and does not reflect truth. Among those who misapprehend the true essence of the Church's faith and mission, are those that wrongly equate maturity with the capacity to accommodate a secularized reading of Scripture and its application in the world. The church shows maturity when she becomes proficient in her response to every segment of society without prejudice or preferential treatment while remaining scriptural. Distortions of faith and mission often lead to a frenzied response to declining membership and communal demands with solutions counterintuitive to divine mandates. In its fear of becoming obsolete, keeping members, recruiting new members, and withstanding the pressure of secularization, some religious entities have relaxed their values and reconfigured God's Word to allow what God denies and jettison what He codifies as essential for relationship with Him.

Some segments of the faith community understandably go to great lengths to preserve God's mandates, by viewing modernity as sacrilegious, and in effect cling to a 1950s model of ministry in a 21st century environment. These see contemporary approaches to ministry (even those not violating Scripture) as a departure from the Faith. Attempting to combat modernity, they fixate on the doctrine of the "One Church" and the interrogatory, 'What must I do to be saved?' even for members who have long since embraced this biblical concept. They outsource other aspects of the church's mission to nonprofits in the community. This model of ministry does not address the phantoms of faith, or real challenges facing people in the pew and public square.

Meanwhile, the onlooker (those unchurched and dechurched) sees the faith community as an entity out-of-touch and irrelevant to the real dynamics playing out behind the scenes in their lives. In their minds, they have not abandoned God but have abandoned traditional forms of church and worship. Hence, the familiar statement "I believe in God and Christ, but not an organized religion or denomination." They continue to search for God and spirituality but do so in unorthodox ways and contexts. They seek actual answers to real questions or resolutions pertinent to their circumstances. These do not see the church as relevant or practical.

The Pew Research Center's study America's Changing Religious Landscape (2015) captures this unfortunate reality. The report highlights that over 100 million people have abandoned traditional forms of the church. The center notes that the Christian share of the population has declined 8% over a 7-year period. In addition, in 2011, David Kinnaman notes that the mosaic group of the population (between ages 18-29) believes the church makes little sense, and they cannot raise their most pressing life questions to the church. The things that concern them most, the church avoids or sweeps under the rug. Subsequently, their quest continues but in the other direction and contexts. In areas in which the church is vocal, mosaics describe the teaching as "shallow."

These findings arouse my attention. I test the findings by examining churches in the Denver Metro area as a small sample. These included not only Churches of Christ but denominational churches and independent churches. An examination of Church websites provides a snapshot of congregational life and their

perception of the community they serve. What was most interesting was how sermons, bible studies and church programs
contrast with issues facing church members and the community.
Most often, there were no signs of correlation between lesson
topics and mundane issues facing members and the community.
For instance, generic topics such as What must I do to be saved,
the church, righteousness and the love of God were frequent.
Whether these lessons adequately respond to hidden issues of
members and the community is debatable. But to an unchurched
person looking for solutions to their challenges, answers are not
clear through these.

I contrast this information with narratives and issues of my former clinical clientele (most of whom identify as Christian) and
those encountered during my former pastoral experience. In
addition, casual conversations with Christians attending church
in this area and through conversations with over 5,000 follow-
ers on social media, over a 4-year period yield information
suggesting that while most people believe the church addresses
their basic issues, the more complex and unorthodox challenges remain unattended. Among these people are some who
feel they cannot raise their issues or concerns about life to the
church they are attending. From this I surmise there is a dis-
connect between religious entities and the more complex and
unorthodox challenges facing parishioners and the surrounding
communities.

In my mind, (at least) this gives credence to Kinnaman's argument about the mosaic group of our population and the findings by the Pew Research Center. Orchestrating and delivering programs and services that meet the needs of the community requires a thorough understanding of the actual issues and questions facing both the church and the community. This reality leads me to write volume one, Hidden Challenges of People of Faith and How to Navigate Them. During this effort, and through intellectual conversations and debate, I surmise the issues facing both those in the church and the community are complex, multifaceted, and protracted sometimes. Subsequently, it became necessary for me to not only create one volume or book but develop a series, hence the series title phantoms of faith developed.

The series exposes hidden challenges of people of faith most often orchestrated by Phantom forces seeking their demise. As examples, the writing highlights narratives of Christians and people of other religions who have experienced challenges in unorthodox contexts, the impact of these on their lives and resolutions. It includes practical perceptions and wisdom regarding unique challenges befalling people of faith and the phantom forces from which they originate. I realize that as Christian and African American writing through the lens of the Western-European culture; the framework presented in this series regarding challenging issues may differ from those living and practicing faith outside my culture. However, I hope this framework provides insight, direction, and resolution for those seeking answers or looking to thwart the forces that undermine

God's intended purpose for their lives. For those looking to improve the quality of their lives and relationships, this can be a resource too. Phantoms of Faith is a series. It is my effort to write each book in this series to honor God and enrich the lives of people across various sectors of life. I hope that this volume and the series will serve as a resource for the church and the unchurched, the minister and the academician, clinicians and counselors, and the religious expert or the novice.

This is my legacy and contribution to the greater good, to the glory of God. In writing this volume I pay homage to ministers, practitioners and scholars for their writing and add to the existing literature with my contribution. This work acts as a reminder to family, friends, and detractors that ultimately it is my acknowledgement of the irrevocable gifts that God has given on me and God's presence in me that makes this scholarship possible. I give all the glory and praise to Him.

-E. D. Allen, D Min. PhD.

Preface to Volume Two (WOMAN)

Humanity's incessant trek, scuff and stretch to prevail, become, and belong is up against a myriad of modalities or negotiations that presents challenges to the church, civilization, individuals, and institutions. One complexity integrated in life's protracted duel is the indispensable existence of the WOMAN. History's canvas exhibit images of the world's perpetual miscarriage of its responsibility and appraisal for Divinity's blessing. Revolving reels of the woman's physical, sexual, and emotional abuse, repeat episodes of neglect, devaluation and self-destruction of the woman dominate the cinema of life. Eve's debacle in the Garden of Eden is a reoccurring nightmare for some of today's women. Like a stubborn cataract, it obscures society's view of her as an essential treasure to adore. Divine adjudication, voices of antiquity and contemporary gatekeepers certify that the plight of the woman is difficult. In their dissent and syndicated efforts to barricade from assault, ease emotional hemorrhage and garner moral restitution, special groups billboard the woman's inhumane experience. But should hallmark of her moral injury, disintegration, her sins, and those perpetuated against her make up the <u>sole</u> concourse leading to restoration, reconciliation, and celebration? What are the constituents of value or worth? This second volume of The Phantoms of Faith series (WOMAN) I attempt to produce a fundamental change that reconstitutes the nexus constructing conventional narratives and outcomes regarding the woman. I decide against assessing her through failure and humanity's catastrophic dealings with her. Instead, I tender a composition that highlights the Creator's imaginative blueprint and architectural processes for the woman. These were evidently essential to producing an exceptional being with beauty, power, and divinity.

This writing attempts to re-appraise integral components of human values; encourage women to be women and extol the Creator for His ingenuity and wisdom manifested in her existence. This is (in my mind at least) a minor effort consequential to restoring and celebrating the woman. Dialogue and analysis of the woman as a powerful constituent to the human experience is imperative. Humanity is derelict if it cannot acknowledge this. We are equally derelict if we fail to showcase phantom forces indiscriminately sifting, pillaging, and disintegrating the lives of women. It then is incumbent of me to include WOMAN as volume II in the Phantoms of Faith series. Since her tenure in paradise the woman is under a perpetual offensive, which is not only the by-product of sin, but an irrefutable concession of her significance to humanity and the plan of God.

The woman is a valuable component and contribution to humanity. In my attempt to showcase her prominence, there are two critical approaches I believe are noteworthy. First, I am cautious not to undermine the integrity, sanctity and tenor of Holy Scripture concerning the woman, or interrogate the unimpeachable motives upon which the Creator's directives and adjudication about her rests. Such a move will evoke Divine repudiation and judgement. (SEE: Duet. 4:2; 12:32; Prov. 30:5-6; Jer. 26:2; Rev. 22:18-19). Second, I politely attempt to deconstruct humanity's narrative and deduction of the woman by focusing primarily on her most pristine state or condition immediately following her creation and disclosure. This shifts the focus of the narrative from the woman to her Creator.

We are uncertain of how much time elapsed between her creation and the events unfolding in the Garden of Eden. Whatever amount of time this is, there is something about this period that displays the mind of God concerning the woman. The woman as a created specialty, the church as an ordained institution and the human experience are better served by this shift.

The Creator's mind concerning the woman and the mission He codifies for her is unequivocal in the Dispensation of Innocence, which is post-creation, the pre-desire, pre-failure, and misappropriation periods during the woman's primal existence. In effect, this book separates out, some precepts usually highlighted in conversations about the woman.

This is not an attempt to minimize or jettison Satan's offensive frequently memorialized through a male malfunction, nor its impact on her and humanity. Valid documentation of the injustice and ill-treatment of the woman in every sector (including the church, to a degree) exists throughout the annals of time.

However, I assert that restoration, reconciliation, and celebration are discoverable through a concourse frequently uncharted. Baring out these three points of agency is productive here. *Restoration* (as chronicled in this writing) is the act of repairing broken pieces, placing something back into its former good condition. Second, what I mean by *reconciliation* is voluntary devotion (by men specifically and society) as an expression of wrong and desire for a proper relationship with the woman. Third, *we target celebration* gratitude, praise, and worship of the Creator for the woman's indelible compliment to humanity. Analysis and discussion about that period in which she is flawless, whole and God focused, lay open leads us down this path. During the interval of her purist state, she is no more or less than what the Creator projects. Her beauty, power and divinity are apparent. If this then becomes the compass navigating the modern woman and the society in which she lives, a critical thoroughfare emerges, which at its end humanity must shout and praise the Creator for the indelible and indispensable creation of the WOMAN.

I hold the conviction that the proverbial quest and squabble over the identity, purpose, and value of the Woman rests at the threshold of greatness, the mind of God. Seeing the Woman through the Eyes of God tilts the narrative into its rightful place and legitimizes her mission and worth. Even with these noble aspirations, writings such as this one will spawn fiery debate from detractors (male and female) opinionated about the bold approach of this writing, its theological implication, social influence, and psychological outcomes.

But the clash of minds is nothing more than sparks generated by iron sharpening iron, a process aimed at a greater good, and a higher calling. Irrespective of today's theological ambiance, social posturing and the consistent debate about the woman, every conversationalist must give the Heavenly Father and Creator His due, by paying homage to Him for the woman, the immutable component of humanity and the grace of life.

-E. D. Allen, D Min. PhD.

Dedication

I dedicate this volume to my grandmother Annie Ruth, whose mind remains sharp at the golden age of 103, and to my mother Gloria, who first introduced me to the Lord during my youth. They are women of strength, women of God.

"If the first woman God ever made was strong enough to turn the world upside down all alone, these together ought to be able to turn it back and get it right side up again."

– SOJURNER TRUTH

Contents

Introduction

As the second volume of the Phantoms of Faith series, WOMAN is recognition of the female's enduring plight during antiquity and contemporary times. It is a sensitive concession of fact, and a composition aimed at promoting healing and attempts to mitigate further moral injury. The book's approach does not pursue conventional paths that billboard and parade the offensive consistently leveraged against her. Rather, it offers a fundamental change to the ideology and way the narrative of the Woman usually exemplifies. Although hints of her inequitable experience in life echoes periodically in the book, the shifted emphasis moves the reader into infrequently charted waters as another route to acceptance, affinity, and applause of the WOMAN.

Instead of distilling narratives from ongoing skirmishes with her male counterpart, the church, her social nexus, and self-perception, divine purpose for the woman's ontological beauty, power, and divinity is the primary theme threaded throughout the book.

This then becomes the book's distinguishing characteristic. It showcases the woman as seen through the Eyes of God, and the purposes for which He created her, and in effect lifts awareness of the fact that the Creator preordained the characteristics and perpetuity of the WOMAN's ontological value. The book invites the reader to lean momentarily out of time and space to capture Divinity's mind and motivation for the creation of the WOMAN. It features the WOMAN as a "created specialty" endowed with a presence and power that reaches far beyond the male's personal utility.

It produces a subtle message to the woman that her proverbial quest to protect her value, elevate her voice, improve her visual equity, and claim victory is already secure, even before the world began. The book crescendos to an ambience of praise and glory for the Creator's infinite wisdom in the WOMAN's creation and reminds everyone that all souls belong to Him and all things subject to His power and purpose.

The indelible beauty of a woman captures the signature of the Lord.

Ishsha

An Indispensable Creation

*I*t is Friday morning, the howling wind rushing through the suburbs of the Mile-High city slices through dense fog, welcoming the dawn of day. As it rustles through the trees, branches beat up against the gutters, which serves as a morning alarm of sorts. Although I would love to rest longer, the nagging sounds and aroma from dark roasted coffee becomes motivation to break out from beneath a warm comforter. While sitting on the side of the bed, the constant drumming of branches against the gutters now serve as a reminder of my to-do-list, behind which a host of other thoughts and concerns emerge. But before allowing these to take my emotions hostage and lead me helplessly throughout the day, I take a moment to pray, give thanks and praise to God for another moment in time and space, for the new kiss of a day uncharted.

The playful sounds emanating from my daughter's room down the hall suspend my ad-hock moment of solitary. Fridays are thrilling for her. Like most, it is her favorite weekday, because

it is an introduction to a weekend of no school, watching videos, trips to movie theaters, parks, restaurants, and church activities with friends! I jump start our daily hustle... we get dressed, grab a quick bite to eat, and then out the door for school and work. After ensuring everyone is where they need to be, and before going up to the office, I make a routine pit stop at one of America's iconic places, the Waffle House. Formed 65 years ago, its mission "to deliver a unique experience, great food, attentive service and a welcoming experience" [1] continue to live as a contemporary aphorism.

Upon entry, the atmosphere introduces customers to a memorable taste of 1960s décor. There is a counter with ten bar stools that protracts in front of the kitchen area. It appears to be the chief attraction in the dining area. The jarring sounds of clanging dishes, the smell of sizzling bacon and a jumping jukebox assaults the senses. Elevated above this organized chaos, the crew greets in one voice, "good morning!" Betty, a seasoned woman, and veteran server is seemingly always up to task when I visit. Amid obvious signs of maturity, glimmers of youth still radiate. Her hair is pulled up with every strand in place, her lipstick and make-up are flawless. As I navigate through the diner, she gathers napkins and eating utensils to meet me at my regular table.

Her gentle sway, gracious spirit, and infectious smile always warms customers as she approaches tables. Good morning hon! Coffee, and then the usual? Yes, I reply. As she scurries back behind the counter to prep the coffee, I pull out my phone to check my email and text my mother "good morning!" Afterwards, I check the news of the day or search for devotional messages to help ensure that the morning continues to move in a good direction. While immersed in emails, Betty brings the coffee to the table. The consistent clanging of dishes distracts me from reading and reminds me to prep my coffee before it is too cold. As I take my first sip, I see through flickering steam and notice a collected group of women, nine of the ten employees working behind the counter. Their symmetry and dissimilarities bare hallmarks of womanhood and highlight a paradoxical praxis that is unquestionably feminine. The diversity between them is apparent. Black, Caucasian, Asian; some are mature, middle-aged and others appear younger; they bare colorful eyeshadow, lipstick, mascara, and big eyelashes; a couple of them favor the natural look. Their hairstyles vary from big curls to bangs and braids, some brandish tattoos on their neck, others on their arms and hands.

What is equally discernible, it seems before leaving home, each of them pays special attention to themselves in a way that stresses their underlining beauty and hosts their unique personalities. In between shouting customer orders to the cook, sporadic dialogue emerges, from which evidence of their innate sensitivities, their aspirations, fears, and failures; their successes, love, and traces of happiness manifests. Betty delicately places my breakfast in front of me. Hot waffles, with maple syrup and butter sliding across like a skier traveling down the ski slopes of Colorado; creamy-buttery grits, sausage and eggs cooked to order, is my coveted southern breakfast of champions. As I dive into this plate of goodness, the restaurant's door chime rings out, and eight people from India walks in.

There are four men and four women, likely couples. As soon as they entered, it was like time halted and the only thing in play was a jamming jukebox in the background. It reminds me of a scene in an old western movie, in which a stranger riding into town on a horse stops at the local saloon. When he enters, the entire saloon stops and stares for three seconds.

The server breaks the awkwardness generated by other customer's curiosity. Good morning! Welcome to the Waffle House! Are you dining in, or will this be to go? Sitting not too far away from the entrance, I can hear them discussing in Hindi whether to dine in or get breakfast to go. Although nowhere near fluent, I am familiar with the culture and their national tongue, which I can identify when I hear it. The traditional twist of the wrist and slight waggle of their heads as they talk is distinctive. A few seconds afterwards, one of them says, "we will dine in, please." The restaurants' hostess yells out, "table for eight!" One table for eight people is challenging in some restaurants like this one. They ended up with two booths, back-to-back to accommodate the group. As they get situated, I notice some of the other guests are still curious about them, understandably. The Waffle House's menu does not feature roti, dosas, idli and chutney, usually; and Indians walking into this kind of diner is not a daily occurrence. After a brief pause, sounds of a busy restaurant return to normal.

As Betty steps over to my table to refill the coffee cup, a cell phone rings out. One of the Indians reaches down into her purse to catch the call. The faint sound of her bangles sliding down her arm is another vivid trait of femininity.

As I look more critically, the brilliant colors of her makeup, attire, and eyebrows flawlessly threaded (as well as the other women accompanying her) are undeniable. Then I realized, women living almost ten thousand miles away in a world and culture undeniably different exhibit distinguishable similarities with those living outside of theirs. It is as if there is a feminine acumen of sorts... a code and language that identifies and coalesces the spirit of womanhood. As I shuffle through the concept, my eyes shift from the Indians seated in the two booths, back to the women working behind the counter, to Betty, who is now engaging the couple seated two tables from me.

Thinking more extensively, I wonder what makes a woman a woman? Who are these lovely creatures? How would people today answer this question? Does the 21st century woman's exposition and exemplification of self define the Woman? Are former First Lady and Icon, Michelle Obama, Oprah Winfrey (Billionaire Media Mogul) and the late Justice Ruth Bader Ginsburg exemplars of the Woman? Will we find the answer embedded in prominent historical events, such as Sojourner Truth's speech, "Ain't I a Woman" delivered at the Ohio Women's Rights Convention in 1851; or like the founding of the National Woman Suffrage Association by Susan B. Anthony, and Elizabeth Cady Stanton in 1869, which was an organization that help pave the way for women's right to vote in 1920? What about the first female Prime Ministers, Indira Gandhi of India, and Margaret Thatcher of Great Britain, do they capture the essence of the Woman? Are the tenets of a woman notable in The Equal Pay Act, signed into law June 10, 1963, by then President John F. Kennedy? Perhaps these are but mere reflections of what has always been. If so, do we surmise they encapsulate the exquisite constituents of the woman

in antiquity? Will then, Agnodice[2] (400 BC) who history recognizes as the first female gynecologist, practicing medicine in Greece during a time when women faced death, illuminate what makes a woman a woman? Maybe Eve, the world's first woman, can enlighten us. Beyond her contribution to the fall of humanity, we know little about Eve. Or do we? Womanhood must have been drastically different before women experienced abuse, devaluation, and subjugation. But what will Eve draw from to give body, vitality, and virtue to womanhood? Whether we get the answer from Eve, or the 21st century woman is irrelevant, when paralleled with the indisputable reality that the woman (like her male-counterpart) is a created being, by a Higher power, God, the Sovereign Creator of the universe.

Mining the Mind of God for Definition of the Woman

This notion ("mining the mind of God") is one we must not conceive lightly or approach carelessly, because it is a precarious suggestion and undertaking. No human, whether the legendary giants of old or 21st century prodigies, has within him capacity for a microscopic dissection of the Holy One, who dwells in unapproachable light. [3] The enormity and complexity of God is such that independent of divine influence, He is beyond human grasp. This then renders the idea impossible. He is immutable and infinitely Supreme in knowledge, wisdom, power, and holiness. Simply stated, He is the epitome of perfection. As the Creator, time and space do not bind Him, because He exists outside its boundaries. There is nothing in creation that can bind Him or miniaturize Him in any form or context. Conversely, the totality of His being is not subject to the parameters or limits of human thinking. Human intellect and philosophy cannot bind or tame Him; nor does He bow to scientific reasoning. We cannot pick His brain (so to speak) or figure Him out, but He reveals Himself to us. Given these, "mining His mind" in this writing can only refer to the delicate reverent process of excavating divine truths and treasures manifest in His word; to which we can never add or detract value and meaning.

What being is more informed than the Creator to give meaning and structure to the woman? Because she did not create herself, she (like the male) is subject to a higher power. Petition any woman to give definition to self and womanhood, she will probably construct and hinge her commentary on critical frameworks. A meaningful Faith usually configures these frameworks. However, the absence of a meaningful faith will also influence her thought process. In addition, are indelible moments (whether heartfelt or traumatic) and the value system and politics that make up her ancestral matrix. Her view of her mother-figure (or the absence of) is a contributing factor; and whether she identifies with or live contradictory to that view. In addition, is the enduring presence or deficiency of a father-figure, and her view of forces working in harmony or in opposition to her aspirations. The woman intricately threads all of these to help frame her thought process, and worldview. But God's view of the woman is far beyond her perception. External stimuli or influence cannot define or confine His motives. He sees everything within the context of His will. His decision-making and influence consistently harmonizes with His divine attributes. Because of this, the woman is likely far greater than even she can define, and certainly beyond that

which is espoused by her male-counterpart. We find the best definition and explanation of the woman within the confines of the mind of God. This point is incredibly significant because God moves and acts in a determined fashion. His absolute sovereignty prevents governing the universe reactively. God predetermines and aligns His will with His divine attributes. He then independently provides the definition and explanation of the woman. She then comes into being and has meaning as determined by God and with no measure of human influence.

She is not, nor could she have been, an afterthought (as some have surmised) or deemed essential only after a review of Adam. The Genesis account details creation as it was unfolding. As best as we can determine, God gave Moses details of these events to record for all of humanity. [4] Not until much later in the Holy Mandate do we learn that the purpose for creation and humanity was ordained "before the foundation of the world". [5] This means that before God called the universe into existence, and obviously, before He created humans, He orders the existence of all things, and that these synchronize with His will. In that moment, God assigns the purpose, identity, and value of both the male and female, and again, with no external influence.

As He begins His work, His only consult is the blueprint in His mind, which He drafts before He utters His voice and moves His hands in the act of creation. Who else was there for Him to consult? What mind is greater than His for Him to seek guidance and approval? God then, at a moment of His choosing, and for reasons determined solely by Him, out of nothing forms critical elements of the universe according to His design.

He moves sequentially, with each act building on the other, reaching that creative summit, a tripartite called man. But it was the woman who becomes the crowning jewel of His creation. Nestled in His thoughts are processes necessary for bringing her to life, and the undefiled tenets of womanhood, that are meted by a theocratic commission and scheme, ensuring she becomes exactly what He intended, an indelible and indispensable act of creation. After fashioning her, the creation process is complete.

An Indelible Creature

Appreciating the powerful notion that God develops the concept of the woman before the world begins requires not only scavenging that period, but creative processes spawning her existence later. There were things created prior to the woman that prove necessary for her existence. Cultural influence and gender bias see this assertion as a viewpoint too difficult to digest. However, it remains fact. Had she come into existence during the violent processes associated with the beginning of creation, He would have made her differently, like angels, who we believe were created by fiat with the universe. [6] Fiat means to command something into existence; to create merely by speaking. It is a divine act beyond the comprehension of finite minds.

Had she existed then, she would be among the first creatures in existence after the beginning of the creation process, the angels. Like them, she would be inconceivably beautiful and engulfed in a glorious radiance too stunning for human eyes to behold. Her body, configured for life outside of this world, would be drastically different. Harnessing incredible powers and ability, the universe would view her differently. But what is even more startling is the shocking realization that her existence during this point of creation would have invalidated womanhood.

Angels, even with all their splendor, intelligence, will, and power, do not have a capacity for elective love, are not relational in the same sense humans are, and given their bodies, they do not have a capacity for reproduction or operate within a family matrix. Because angels are gender-neutral[7], Eve would not have been the "Mother of All Living". Unique compassion, partnership and other sensitivities that make up femininity would have been beyond reach. Simply put, the Woman would not exist. Given these, it is of no wonder that God's concept, creation, and advent of the woman is strategic. God reserved her as the crowning jewel of creation, to step into a significance, mission, and identity predetermined by Him. The insoluble fact God is immutable; and whatever He commissions is unalterable, makes the woman His created specialty, and the value He assigns to her irreducible. We cannot improve the intangible things of creation or destroy them.
They are independent and indefinite, in effect. For instance, since its inception, energy cannot be re-created or destroyed. We can only convert or transport energy. [8]

In addition (and apart from God) life is the most valuable, guarded, and coveted possession among people. Irrespective of the quality of one's human experience, the preservation and pursuit of life is a vivid testament to its absolute value. The memorable and haunting age of the COVID-19 pandemic bares out this. Likewise, we cannot alter the true value of the woman by human influence or situational matrix. She can choose to live in harmony or in contradiction of said value; or powerful, debilitating, and subjugating forces in her environment can affect the quality of her human experience, but they cannot influence the value God has assigned to her. Regardless of what happens to her or what she does, she is still a WOMAN, whose value and identity is inherent.

This reality is not (in any way) denial or minimization of her sins, or the ill-treatment and injustice levied against her throughout the annals of time, nor its spiritual effects, sociological measures, psychological outcomes, and economic impact. Conversely, it attests that her God-given excellencies are irreducible. The human experience can only influence the quality of her life, never those divinely imposed essentials of womanhood. These inalienable merits of womanhood are notable in the very act of her creation. This is the premise for all God codifies for her and the source from which humanity should draw and synchronize its appraisal of her in scientific, social, and spiritual contexts. Given that society cannot determine her authenticity and value, investigating her introduction to the world is meaningful.

The creation of the woman notably dawns in succession to a series of divine events, i.e., after God secures the foundations of the universe, behind manipulating the earth's environment into a suitable habitat for humans, and after the creation of her counterpart- Adam, and then following the formation of animals, in varying categories. [9] Her place in the sequence of the creation event is not a contingency diminishing her value or significance at all. In fact, it stresses the opposite. Presumably,

God makes the best of creation at the end of the process. An elevated state of readiness was necessary for her reception. She could not exist before the world was ready to receive the gift of God. When He begins the process for creating the first humans, there are two notable seismic shifts that unfold:

1) Irrespective of everything created by Him, He directly and intentionally creates humans after His image and likeness. This act alone creates a chasm between man and the animal kingdom.

2) For the first time, God does not create via fiat, but has a more intimate involvement in the process and creates with His hands. At no point during His creation of Adam and Eve does He speak.

When God creates humans, He starts with the man, by taking dust from the ground. Today's science confirms that the same elements found in dust are in human DNA[10].

In addition, we know DNA comprises genetic material with coded information determining the nature, growth, and life of an organism; and has the extraordinary capacity to diagnose, repair, and reproduce.[11] Given genetic studies recently conducted, we now know that as God creates Adam, He installs approximately one thousand million bits of information in the cells that make up his body. He is (in part) defined by these. At the point of his creation, God provides everything necessary for Adam to be what He ordains, a man. After the Lord finishes creating Adam, He brings him to life and places him in the Garden of Eden. Among the tasks given to him is the daunting project of naming all the animals. But if you follow the text, after God determines it is "not good for man to be alone", He brings the animals to Adam for him to identify.

The critical aspect of this statement is too often lost to hollow human perception, which interprets this as a divine concession of an oversight, an oops (if you will). But far be it from the Creator, who does not make mistakes or over looks anything, and nothing surprises. Gathering and parading animals before Adam was not to correct an error, but to lift awareness of man's earthly mission ordained by his Creator. It is a novel commission that includes a collaborative effort with a unique partner. It was never God's intention for Adam to operate independently, but in concert and stereo with a created specialty. The Creator wants Adam to appreciate what He was about to do, and who He was placing in his care. He wants him to understand his limitations and note the differences between man and woman.

Now, that indelible act etched in the mind of the Creator before the foundation of the world is precisely for this moment. He places Adam into a "deep sleep", that realm of unconsciousness that temporarily divorces humans from experiential knowledge, unplugs the brain from signals and reflexes to pain. This move declares and introduces the world's first master anesthesiologist and chief surgeon, God. But there are no surgical beds, intravenous drip of propofol, surgical knives or instruments. There is no one present to hand Him a scalpel, because Registered Nurses and Surgical Techs do not exist. There are no medical residents in training, for this work is only God's.

Where the Creator pulls off His next creative masterpiece is notably distinctive. He creates Adam from dust outside Eden, but the woman comes into being in a lush paradise. Many others will probably surmise that this distinction is insignificant. However, it bears noting that God could have grabbed another handful of dust to create Eve immediately following His creation of Adam, but He did not. We must appreciate the timing and significance of the creation of the woman. The text does not show that God gave Adam any warning or requires preparation for surgery. It only says, "God caused a deep sleep to fall upon the man." [12] In this moment, with the gentle sounds of pure river waters running in the background, while birds ballet in the heavens, and as animals roam about, and a curious angelic host looks on, God (with nothing but His mind and hands) surgically cuts into Adam's side. Now, this is where the narrative becomes intriguing and profoundly complicated.

God takes (according to the English translation) a rib from Adam to create the woman. [13] There are many theological narratives regarding how this part of the body correlates with the perceived role of the woman. Although I will not indulge these here, the fact God could have elected any other part of the body or created her out of any other material is noteworthy.

But irrespective of the historical, theological ambience surrounding the woman's role in this context, I choose the route infrequently charted during most discussions about this divine event. Most people picture God taking one rib out of Adam to create Eve. In fact, some have wondered whether men have fewer ribs than women. The answer is no. Contemporary science confirms that if the periosteum (the membrane surrounding bones) is intact while removing a rib, the bone will grow back. Perhaps this is the reason men are not missing a rib today. Others surmise that women have more ribs than men, which is also incorrect.

The Hebrew word used for a rib in the Genesis account, notably, translates as "side". A proper exegesis of the text reveals that God not only took a rib from Adam, but a piece of his side, including flesh, tissue, nerves, blood, and DNA. I will come back to the subject of DNA and its significance to this writing later. But for now, it is important to point out that with Adam's DNA, the Creator does something strikingly different in His creation of the woman. The text says that God "formed man from the dust of the ground" and all the animals additionally. The Hebrew word used for "form" connotes the molding process a potter uses to form clay into a jar or vase. But there is a noted shift when creating the woman.

God does not include dust (at least, not directly) in the blueprint for her, and it is not the key element in her creation. The Hebrew word for fashioned, as used in this text about the woman, is literal. It means to build. God moves to a distinct part of the garden and builds or constructs the woman. That He moved to a different section of the garden may appear insignificant. However, it stresses the notion (in my mind, at least) that man did not take part in the woman's creation. Further, the inability and absence of the woman's opinion and influence over her creation is equally noteworthy.

Again, independent of human influence, God builds the woman. Building something requires special material. As we know, processes involved in constructing almost anything are multiphasic, intricate, and require varying dimensions, estimates, specific frames, structures, and foundations. Special attention goes into the making of the woman, a fact comparatively obvious.

As He builds the woman, God embeds His Spirit and nurturing characteristics unique to her, and installs wisdom, strength, and capacity for intelligence, skill, and a measure of love far beyond her counterpart's ability. She carries a greater element of divinity within her. God endowed her with grace and tenderness that helps mitigate life's tumultuous experiences. Nestled in her soul is a constellation of sensitivities that forms a paradoxical nexus that simultaneously strengthens and makes her vulnerable. Like a rare priceless jewel, she is both valuable and adorable, for which her protection by humanity is mandatory. Uniquely beautiful, she is unlike anything in creation. The Creator has entrusted her with the responsibility and capacity to reproduce and cultivate life. This is a high calling and honor that is only hers. Sometimes, God, for His own will and purpose, has relieved some women of this responsibility, even though they may desire it. But a woman is a woman not because her society, environment and family matrix declare it, but because her DNA commands she should be, belong and become. God coded all components that determine womanhood into her DNA. This explains why women living ten thousand miles apart exhibit similar attributes. The simplest way to understand this is to understand that DNA is primarily about information storage and retrieval. [14] Contemporary science confirms that every living organism has within its genetic information informing that organism not only to exist, but how to function as they are.[15]

The Evergreen tree is green year-round because there is information telling it to remain green; the red rose is red because of the genetic information instructing it to be so. A fish will never walk or talk because the coded information in its DNA does not enable capacity to walk and talk. Similarly, the sensitivities, tenderness, the gracious spirit, mannerisms, neurological tendencies, anatomical structure, and complexities innate to the woman are codified by her DNA. God embedded her identity, purpose, and value in her genetic code. This is the premise, and fact from which I extrapolate the assertion that the value, purpose, and identity of the woman develops independent of human influence and is irreducible by any external stimuli.

However, many people process the negative aspects of the woman's human experience as a force capable of reducing or expunging her identity, and the estimates or value imprinted in her by the Creator. The negative aspects of her human experience only affects her psychology, meaning the mental and emotional outlook formed by an erroneous and diminishing appraisal of her identity and worth, or sometimes, the sheer absence of these. Whether her male counterpart or some other aspect of her community discharges this estimate, the efficacy of pain, denial, and delimitation, will hoodwink and bamboozle her opposition into thinking that it is okay to treat her less than what God intends. They deceive themselves, in effect. The notion that they can alter the woman's original being, and value is a *formal fallacy.* [16] The core identity and value of a woman cannot change, it is immutable. One may foolishly choose not to honor it, or behave oppositionally, but such forces cannot change what God has done. However, abuse, neglect, minimization, and subjugation perpetuated by her environment causes actual injuries, which affect her psychology of herself and the world she sees.

The one thousand million bits of information lodged in her cells configure her existence to God's blueprint. She needs nothing else to be what God created her to be, a woman. The Creator gave everything necessary for this aim to her. The things setting her apart from her counterpart, and that uniquely define her, are the very things that make her suitable for the man, and the right additive and specialty for God's plan for humanity. If a man is king, she is his crown. The lion might be king of the jungle, but the lioness (more agile and faster) hunts for prey. As noted biblically, she is the glory of the man. The notion that the woman is God's stellar act of creation, and an indelible gift to humanity, is an indisputable fact throughout time. Meanwhile, on the other side of the garden, the Creator finishes this masterpiece. She (like Adam) stands before the Creator in perfect form and is flawless; yet, lifeless, until God breathes into her. We are not privy to whether there was a conversation between God and Eve before meeting Adam or whether she understood what was happening next. The text only notes that God "... brought her to the man."[17]

Even this idea is significant! He does not send her to the man; he brings her to him. It is not wise to leave something valuable and precious unguarded and unattended. In addition, the gesture connotes divine bestowal, a personal gift, a cherished treasure, like a father walking his daughter down the aisle to present and give away the one valuable to him. Although taken from man, Divinity's presentation of her is a silent but powerful statement, that she is a special work of His hand, a gift from His heart, and manifestation of His divine providence. We must view this as a WARNING! Because every perfect gift originating from God's love, holiness, and sovereignty[18] demands admiration and gratitude. Failure to do this dishonors the Lord as Creator and dis-affirms His providential care of His creation.

Ishsha, an Indispensable Creation

We do not know when, or how, God brings Adam back into consciousness. The text does not provide this information. We are unaware if it happens before God arrives with Eve for Adam, or some other point. It would not be implausible that as he looked across the garden, the woman pleasantly surprises Adam, as he sees her coming toward him in such grace and thunder. In whatever way it unfolds, can you imagine what Adam is thinking? He awakes from a deep sleep; he did not know was coming (and may not have fully understood) to find standing in front of him, not only his Creator, but this other creature, who is of the same species, yet drastically different.

What she may have thought or said to Adam is unknown to us. If she spoke, her voice alone would have likely produced a strikingly soft sound that made Adam melt from the inside out. Stunningly beautiful, she causes his brow to raise. His soul flips inside of him. Adam's response notably captures the effect of God's presentation of the woman. He states, "This is now bone of my bone, flesh of my flesh...". [19] The English translation of this phrase does not adequately capture Adam's genuine sentiment. The Hebrew renders this phrase as a poem of sorts, a poetic phrase presented as a short song. The world's first love song is about a woman.

Although he is only a few hours old, Adam is beside himself as he beholds and engages the most beautiful creature he has ever laid eyes on. Eve is a few minutes old; she is brand new, flawless. Never again in the expanse of time will humans lay eyes on, or experience another as pristine as Eve. Because, immediately following the fall of man, the world, and everything in it decays gradually, including the human body and mind.

To appreciate these notions, and Adam's reaction to Eve, remember, before being made unconscious he was just finished surveying lions, tigers and bears, and elephants and hippos romping around. Eve was a healing sight for sore eyes. When expounding this narrative, many people interpret Adam's response to Eve as solely physical attraction. Some see this as a type of lust, which it is not. There are a couple of factors that place these events in proper context:

> One: God creates Adam and Eve as mature adults. They are exempt from the normal processes of development we know. The only thing undeveloped in them was their spirituality and relationship with God, which is in the making. Their maturity suggests that they had within them everything necessary for the other, and for effective relationship. Eve, as a woman, is everything Adam needs as a man; and he as a man is everything Eve

needs as a woman. Together they are exactly what God ordained for His earthly agenda.

Second, although they meet initially in stark nakedness, Adam's excitement and interest does not derive from lust, or solely about the woman's body. Remember, the Eden event occurs during the dispensation of innocence.

He knows nothing about lust at this point. In fact, neither Adam nor Eve is aware of their nakedness or feel any shame associated with this state. It is not until after their fall they develop inappropriate sexual thoughts, guilt, and shame. [20] In this context, the woman's body extends the innate sensitivities and qualities embedded in her just a short while ago. For instance, a woman's hair exhibits her glory, and her smile and voice are reflections of a tender spirit, most often.

A woman can carry herself in such a way that showcases her inner sensitivities. The other important truth associated with their nakedness is that it is emblematic of the human's intrinsic value. Have you noticed, we enter the world naked and when we leave; we do so empty-handed? We bring nothing into the world, and we take nothing out. [21] Why can we not take anything from this world to the next? The world does not and cannot add value to humans. True elements of value are intangible. We do not find the best of the human experience in possessions or empty experiences, but in those things that promote and reflect the Creator. The spirit of joy and peace, acts of love and kindness, mercy, forgiveness, and the image of God are absolute composites of human value. These usually inundate the woman's personality. In contrast to what he has already experienced, Adam likely encounters or picks up on the tenderness of a woman, which influences how he interprets her. After breaking into a joyful, poetic phrase, he identifies her with a name that captures the essence of her being.

The Hebrew bible notes Adam's words as "this one shall be called Woman. Because she was taken out of Man." [22]

Through this name, he captures the uniqueness of the woman's creation (not from dust) and he captures the essence of her being. The Hebrew root for Man is "Ish". But the Hebrew root for Woman is "Ishsha", which means soft. Adam's first impression of the woman is not only that she is beautiful, but soft. His interpretation of Eve certifies the delicacy and preciousness of a woman. Her softness is not about weakness, but shows she is a created specialty.

Now that God exposes the world to His gift, the Woman, there is no turning back. She is an indelible act of creation, imprinted into humanity. Given all the tenderness, sensitivities, strength, skill, intellect, and wisdom God has placed in her and the divine responsibilities equally imposed, she is indispensable. Life without the Woman would be hollow and catastrophic. The human experience would become rough around the edges. In fact, without her, Adam would be still romping around with animals in the garden, because there would be no reproduction. She is the vessel of life. Like Adam, she is among the only aspects of God's creation made in His image.[23]

But there is one exception, God gave her a greater capacity to love. When the world sees the Woman through the eyes of her Creator, they behold and embrace a precious specialty, a gift of love that, as noted, we must respect and admire to His glory and praise. God settled the persistent squabble across cultures regarding the value and identity of the Woman before the world began. Because God created her as a special unit in His plan, she is uniquely valuable. Although the Woman carries a special element of divinity (love) within her, she is not God in and of herself. Like her counterpart, she is subject to a Higher power. The male and female are to live in harmony with the Creator, individually and collectively. The essence of the Woman is so special, the Proverb writer notes, "He who finds a wife finds a good thing. And obtains favor from the Lord." Proverbs 18:22.

When appreciating the Woman thru the eyes of the Creator, we can only surmise that she is a valuable entity, a unique blessing indispensable to humanity. Contrary to modern perception, the Woman's ability to shatter glass ceilings, mediated through her corporate status, her portfolio, entrepreneurship, or an Oscar, does not determine her value, beauty, and power; nor does the MD, JD., or PhD. behind her name. Whether she wields a forklift or tractor-trailer better than her male-counterpart and can match or outperform him in any other category, is less important in the grand scheme of divinity. While these are noble aspirations and skill sets that are within her rights and reach, and which she can assume at will, the Woman's value, beauty, and power are clear and magnified when she steps into the excellence and significance for which God created her. The most beautiful and powerful woman is the one who aligns with her inner divinity. Godly wisdom becomes her beauty, and the fear of the Lord is her power. She exhibits a type of gracefulness that commands a room. Even when her voice is silent, she

speaks. Her behavior is influential, her love nurtures, rebuilds and directs. Humanity is better served by encouraging the woman's existence. We can do this together by ensuring she has a place, a voice and opportunity to affect humanity in the way and extent God intends. When we as people do this, we honor and glorify God as Creator.

Look closely, and you will find reflections of God in the eyes of a woman.

The Ontology of She

Being and Becoming to Belong

1065 BC, in a mountainous region 8 miles southeast of an Israeli city called Hebron, is a town historically known as Maon. [1] The annals of holy antiquity tell us that this small town once hosted a woman named Abigail and her family. The community knew her for her intelligence and beauty. [2] Her gracious inner spirit and striking beauty would even make a respected King bow in admiration. Her intelligence was equally noted and respected in the community. Abigail married an extraordinarily rich man, who most people knew as an evil, obnoxious scoundrel, and drunken egotist. Most of his interactions with people in the community were rude, insensitive, and barbaric. He lived in stark contrast to his wife. Given how exquisite Abigail is, and how beastly her husband behaves, it is not surprising to see the couple as a type of "beauty and beast". During this period not only was a massive accumulation of the local currency a measure of a man's wealth, but gold, silver, animals, property, and large amounts of land.

The couple owned three thousand sheep and one thousand goats on land 2.5 miles away in Mount Carmel. The massive livestock usually kept Abigail's husband busy attending to them or cutting business deals with markets nearby. Bedouins usually inundate the area in which their land is situated. with Bedouins, are bands of Arabs who often raided livestock, land, and other property. Close to their land were caves in which a noted king and his army used as an impermanent residence. People throughout Israel knew the king as mighty, an expert in warfare, and one who commands a fierce army. He was a leader behind whom the Hand of God rests. It was not uncommon for him to decapitate a man for his sins, crimes, or injustices. The people respected his lordship.

In fact, on occasions, while engaged in ordinary conversations with him, some of his subjects would stand before him, trembling. Israel was the superpower of that day, in which this king is a fierce ruler. Other kings and heads of state in faraway places trembled at the mere mention of him. He was a powerful force during this period.

The king was aware of the Bedouins that terrorized and devastated landowners in the area. While temporarily housed near Abigail's family land, he employs his fierce army to protect landowners from Bedouins. They formed a wall around the land day and night. In addition, given their proximity to the land, some of the family's employees routinely interacted with the king's army, who treated the men very well.

One evening, sounds of hired men shearing sheep on their land drifts through the wilderness to where the king and his men are situated. He sends ten of his men to collect compensation for protecting the family's land and livestock. When they approach Abigail's husband, as usual, he is grumpy, rude, and insensitive. He rejects their request, and although the king is popular and revered throughout the country, he pretends he does not know who he is, which is dishonoring, and adds insult to injury.

The men return to give the king an update, in which they convey the exact words and sentiment of Abigail's husband. Meanwhile, one shearer runs to Abigail to inform her of the husband's actions. The man knew what might happen as a result, and that the husband's harsh mannerism made it difficult to talk to him. After hearing the news, and likely while the king's men were in debrief with him, Abigail jumps up... and rushes to prepare something to give the king and his men. She knew well that he would ride in and destroy her husband, family, employees, and their livestock. She knew God was with this king. Her heart is racing because she knows she has little time.

Hurrying about, she does not speak to her husband about his stupidity. Her mind is on her family, their livelihood, and the innocent lives of herdsmen employed by her husband. Besides, given his temperament, she knows he will take issue with her efforts, and attempt to deny her the opportunity. Death is certain behind such a move. Abigail's wisdom is spot-on. Because, as she quickly prepares something for the king, he is in debrief with his men. After hearing that the husband will not honor his request, he summons four hundred of his men to grab their weapons, mount up, and ride. Mission: to destroy totally, leaving no man alive.

Abigail prepares as much as she can and quickly rides off to intercept the king and his army. Given the urgency, it is likely that she lashed her horse to move at full throttle. As the animal kicks up dust and pebbles, she realizes she cannot outrun the king's mighty army. Knowledgeable of the area, she takes a shortcut to intercept them. Her adrenaline is up... she is stressed because she must get to him, before he gets to her family, otherwise, it is over!

The band of warriors the king summonsed into action were not chewing flatbread or sipping wine as they rode. This was a fierce army. The king has issued a command. They are moving with intent. Four hundred horses rapidly galloping across the wilderness creates a distinctive sound, which is likely audible well before their arrival. As she closes in on them, the faint sound of horses thundering across the land grows increasingly louder. Making her way down the hidden trail in the mountain, she sees the king leading his army from a distance. She rushes into their path. As she approaches, she finds that the narrative is true; the king is handsome and strong in appearance, and the men behind him, strapped with weapons, are mighty indeed. Their appearance is intimidating.

Regardless, she dismounts her donkey before it comes to a complete stop. The king commands his army to pause. What Abigail does next, become a defining act and moment for her, her family, the king, and his valiant warriors. Her beauty, power and divinity are apparent through her actions.

First, although Abigail is immensely beautiful, she does not bat her eyes, soften her voice, or sway her hips more intensely to mitigate the righteous indignation of the king. But Abigail immediately falls to her knees and prostrates her face toward the ground. She addresses the king as, "my lord." Even though this type of greeting and mindset will probably cause the 21st century woman to cringe, it is an indelible act of humility, a notable confession of error, and a powerful concession of God's providence.

Her response to rank and authority is not the only evidence of her humility, but a sacrificial spirit highly visible in this context. After greeting the king, she says, "put the blame on me alone." Translation: take my life, not my family's or the innocent men working on our behalf; please do not destroy our land. Abigail's sole purpose for rushing to intercept the king and his army is to offer herself as a sacrifice, a reservoir for the devastation now warranted behind her husband's fatal error. In her mind (at least) such a sacrifice would protect her family from destruction. It is through this selfless act that she present humility as the first impression of her beauty.

Humility can manifest in sacrifice as self-denial. It is born out of the recesses of love. In Abigail's case, she displayed it as an attitudinal adjustment that understands that the good of the many supersedes the needs of one individual. This was not something Abigail created or grasped in the moment; but is obviously of the fabric of her being. It is who she is... and by being; she becomes... she becomes what is desperately necessary for the moment. She stresses this when the hired hand reaches out to Abigail regarding the emerging crisis. His actions

WOMAN: Beauty-Power-Divinity in Motion

are a concession that her reputation in the community positions her as a suitable antidote to the looming problem.

Second, she makes a confession of error by pleading with the king to pardon her husband's moral deficiency. It is an exemplar of her intellect regarding moral law and the principles of governance imposed in her country. As noted, she is intelligent. What is even more noteworthy is she is processing all of this under duress yet remains in control of her emotions and the critical situation at hand.

Third, and likely the most significant of the three, the way she approaches the king is a concession of the God behind him. A godly woman will always see her Creator/God behind and beyond the man. He (God) then becomes the driving force behind her decision-making and subsequent behavior. Abigail knew well that crossing a king anointed by God crosses Him, a fact wholly absent in the mind of her foolish husband. She lets the king know she is aware of who he is, his mission and the power of God who sustains him.

Abigail touches the King's heart. He finds her knowledge and in-depth discernment impressive. Listening intently, he accepts her plea and decides against pursuing his mission. The king extols God for using Abigail to mitigate a brutal attack. He accepts Abigail's gifts, sends her back to her home without harm.

As Abigail returns home, her husband (who is clueless that his wife has just averted death and destruction) has thrown a party and is sloppy drunk. Deciding not to engage him while he is intoxicated, she walks past him and the other men without saying a word. Fatigued from the day's tumultuous events, she turns in for the evening. But when morning dawned and after the alcohol has retreated from her husband's mind and body, she discloses details of the events the day before. Holy antiquity tells us that upon receiving this news, "his heart died within him so that he became like stone." Translation: he suffered a heart attack and a stroke! Ten days later, God takes his life. [3]

Ontology and the Woman

You are likely wondering, what does an antiquated anecdote have to do with women living in the 21st century? What do horses, goats, and sheep have to do with Mercedes, Corvettes, and a 9 to 5 at the office? Like any other form of history, old narratives facilitate and improve appreciation of unique dynamics and processes that make up the human experience; it provides knowledge and wisdom and helps increase appreciation of contemporary events. Biblically, old narratives provide learning and spawn hope for those living today. [4] The narrative about Abigail exhibits ontology that is commensurate to today's woman. As mentioned, similarities between women from different eras highlight and validate the notion that the critical essentials of womanhood are innate. Cultural influence, nuances, beliefs, and dynasty are arguably major contributors to the contemporary woman's thoughts, social needs, and her being. But this assertion (that is, the ontology of women in antiquity, validate the essentials of womanhood today) is likely met with cynicism and criticism, given that the ambience and legitimacy of freedom calls for one to create their own path and draw their own conclusions to life's experiences.

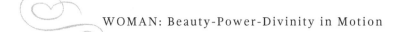

However, context and experience do not create new essentials or characteristics of one's ontology, but invite us to lean into our core self, and become who we are, in effect. It is an act of self-discovery and development, as opposed to a new composition of being. I am speaking of the "newness" one surmises or declares after experiencing a life-altering encounter, for example, "After going through this difficult period, I am a new person, said Joann."

But in this chapter, new does not refer to "another", or that which is quantitatively different, but qualitatively the "other". For example, the dress purchased from Macy's for Mother's Day 2020 is quantitatively and qualitatively new compared to the dress purchased from Dillard's in December for Christmas 2019. It is new quantitatively and qualitatively because it is another.

But when something is qualitatively the other, or qualitatively new, its quality becomes the defining measure, and creates the perception of "another" or a different one, when in fact it is the same entity or person. If a couple renovates their residence, it will look and feel like a "new" place. What causes this perception and emotion? Quality causes the emotional shift. The improvements or changes made to their home create a sense of newness, when in fact it is the same residence merely functioning by design. The same is true if you refurbish a car's engine and paint, it will present and feel "like new", when in fact it is the same automobile presenting and functioning by design. Good quality is the "other" of poor quality.

That context and experience do not create new essentials and characteristics is one that rotates on a dual axis, which encompasses two principles I have dubbed here as the creation principle and the cyclical principle. The creation principle refers to those unalterable forms and impossibilities authored and fixed by the Creator during the creation event series. One example is the sky (the heavens or expanse) which was formed during creation and fixed to always function by design. The same sky suspended over the Garden of Eden thousands of years ago is the same sky you and I look up to every day. It is impossible to move or alter. The second example of the creation principle is innate sensitivities and qualities embedded and born out of the woman's DNA. The genetic code the Creator imprinted in the woman's DNA gives her meaning, purpose and value, which is immutable at the molecular level. [5] One can contradict and deny it socially, spiritually and in other aspects of life, but its origin and foundation can never be altered.

The second axis and principle around which this idea rotates is what I call the cyclical principal. I based this point on the biblical truth that there is nothing new in life, a notion extracted from a biblical passage about the cyclical nature of life.

> That which has been is that which will be, and that which has been done is that which will be done. So, there is nothing new under the sun. Is there anything of which one might say, see this, it is new? Already it has existed for ages which were before us.
>
> Ecclesiastes 1:9-10 (NASB)

Given these two principles then, life contexts and experiences do not innovate ontology, but call us into fundamental structures that help us navigate human affairs.

What is ontology? The definition varies and depends on the theme or context. For example, ontology is a part of mathematics, medicine, knowledge management and data science, to name a few. Rather than exploring these to extract meaning, I only note its philosophical origins that lends itself to our discussion. In this view, ontology is the investigation of the essence of being, becoming, or one's existence and reality. It technically derives from metaphysics and highlights similarities and differences between those things that exist. [6] It asks, what is there or what is fundamental?

However, my approach is more contemporary, meaning psychological and spiritual, and asks, what does it mean to be a woman? What does it mean to be at all? People usually prefer to fill in this blank themselves or give their own meaning of what it is to be. We carved these definitions out of human experiences and aspirations, those attained already and those still unrealized. Their principles of meaning are likely structured in a way that gives liberty to be and become in whatever way one surmises; and belong to what one chooses, rather it is wrong or right, spiritually sanctioned, or culturally acceptable. In her persistent effort to escape misogyny and devaluation, the woman notoriously adapts this view and process to extract meaning. But male or female, how does one who has never been know how to be or exist meaningfully?

We cannot overemphasize the notion that the Creator did not create humans to leave us unattended and on our own to figure out how to be and become. Life has meaning far beyond the human experience, and the individual desires and perceptions born out of it. As noted, these do not give the woman meaning, and the does not determine the true essence of a man; yet the existence of the one gives birth to differentiation of the other. Because Adam was, Eve could not be the same. She had to be different. I do not mean we should view or treat the woman inferiorly, but that she is distinct. Equality must extend past its cultural meaning, which is better understood by delicately sifting through the true principles of being. Again, human inclination will prefer to define what these principles should be. Although the Creator has given us will, the right to choose, life's true meaning must still include those things described and demanded by Him.

In my effort to highlight and lay out principles of being (especially as it relates to the woman) Immanuel Kant (1724-1804) is a valuable source for reflection. Kant was a renowned German philosopher noted for his stellar, comprehensive, and systematic works in the philosophical principles of beauty, moral principles governing individual behavior, and metaphysics, which is a branch of philosophy that deals with the first principles of things, such as being, knowing, identity, time, and space. Kant's work included epistemology; a theory of knowledge that investigates what distinguishes belief from opinion. As impressive and influential as Kant's work was, the principles escalating from his work are not a substitute for Scripture but highlight the Holy Mandate, its truths, competence, and influence on the human-divine relationship.

Given that God is Creator, the source and definition of good, and the epitome of righteousness, I would argue that the etiology of Kant's principles, or concepts driving them, derives from the Creator.

Kant's research and scholarship categorizes one version of what it means to be, which ironically captures the theme of this chapter (that is) one's ontology is not self-defined, nor rise solely from human experience; but emanate from the interior of God's mind, from which the definitive codes and imprints our DNA originates. Kant's view acknowledges that the human mind has intrinsic organizing principles that provide capacity for evaluating human experience. I am cognizant of inconsistencies within Kant's approach, and that other noted scholars challenge Kant's view. However, his observations that note and points to a higher intelligence as the sole origin of the characteristics of being as defined by him, is in sync with the tenor of this writing, and is noteworthy in this context, if no other. Kant touted 12 categories of being, which he deconstructs in four divisions. [7]

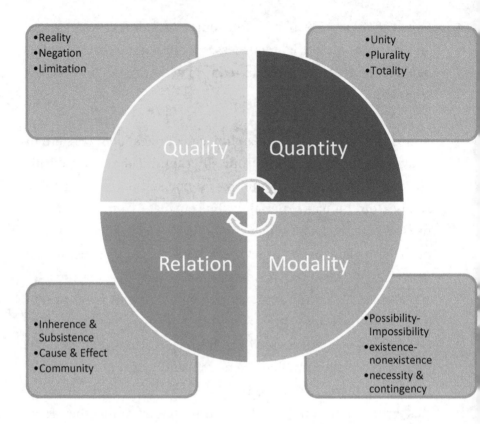

•Reality
•Negation
•Limitation

•Unity
•Plurality
•Totality

Quality   Quantity

Relation   Modality

•Inherence &
 Subsistence
•Cause & Effect
•Community

•Possibility-
 Impossibility
•existence-
 nonexistence
•necessity &
 contingency

One of the most important factors taken from this view is the notion that the categories of being are innate, and not garnered through human experience. Human experience leads to self-discovery, discovery of intrinsic treasures and properties of being. These categories are data about how to be, belong and become. If we surmise this data is innate, where did it come from? This question takes us back to previous discussion regarding data imprinted by the Creator in human DNA, and that such data informs a person how to be, to belong and become.

This brings another concept to mind, which is the innate nature of these characteristics; and if they are innate, we must contribute both their origin and immutability to the Creator.

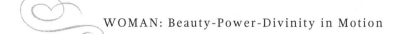

Immutability implies that these characteristics do not change or develop over time; the principals defining them are unalterable. The characteristics of being are a part of the "creation principle" noted above. A complete understanding of the notion that these derive from the Creator requires analysis of Trinitarianism (the teaching that God exists in three persons, but is one being) which is a complicated study too exhaustive to broach in its entirety here. However, I will say, after God forms the universe, He had to establish a medium by which His created order could relate and bridge the infinite chasm between Him and His finite creatures, humans.

Because it is important for us to understand God's mission regarding His creation, He identifies as God the Father, Son and Holy Spirit, through whom His divine attributes mediate. But for His creatures to know Him, to respond, communicate and experience Him through divine communion, in both this life and the hidden world to come, it was necessary for Him to embed a part of Himself in the creature to effect relationship. There had to be a medium and a link through which thought and sentiment could flow between the creature and the Creator. He designated these same characteristics of being for not only relationship with Him, but relationship between humans to a lesser extent.

Science determined long ago that humans are social beings, born wired for communication, bonding, and relationship; and that we desire love, affirmation, and need to express the same. We know that these are in our DNA. For instance, John Bowlby (1907-1990) a renowned psychologist, psychoanalyst, and psychiatrist, recognized for developing the attachment theory, held that human's need for relationship is innate. Bowlby's theory of attachment teaches that humans are pre-programmed to form attachments with others as a survival mechanism. [8] The absence of meaningful relationship during critical moments of human development and life itself will lead to impairment or worse, death.

When we enter and live through the natural course of development, our need for and capacity to embrace and lean into these characteristics of being is immutable. Instances in which these characteristics cannot mature within an individual, psychological injury, or neurological deformity are culprits. But when the body forms naturally, there is an intrinsic presence and need for these characteristics of being, the reality of which gives credence to Kant's argument. Emphasis on these as something intrinsic really highlights the fact that they derive from the Creator. This detail presents three notable conclusions:

> 1) Given that these traits emanate from Him, they integrate into His essence, and by essence, I mean the indispensable and unchanging properties, which serves to identify Him. For instance, the bible states in I John 4:8, God is Love. What this means is that love is not just a feature of His character but is the nature of His being; it is a primitive state of condition, untouched and uninfluenced by any external entity, power or being. God is love, not because it originates from some other source. His loving nature is constantly and consistently self-sustained, self-generated, and self-regulated. Therefore, given this, our knowledge of love originates from Him only.

By this, He is the expression and example of love. Humanity's original capacity to not only identify love, but express it, correlates to the information embedded in Adam and Eve's DNA, which is passed on through reproduction. Remember, God created Adam in His image and likeness; and the infrastructure for Eve's DNA came from Adam, making both male and female like the Creator.

2) Having originated from God, these traits are teleological. By teleological, I mean that the characteristics of being are born out of divine purpose, which is perfected by supreme intelligence and wisdom. When God embedded the characteristics of being into human DNA, it was purpose driven and goal oriented; because there was something God was looking to achieve by giving humans the essence of being. The mere thought of which provides deeper meaning to the biblical phrase, "... man became a living soul."

Reiterating again, Scripture and science clarify that human are social beings, and with inherent capacities to facilitate connection, interaction, and emotion. In short, because He is a relational being, God made us with the capacity for relationship both with Him, and to a lesser extent, each other. Our relationship with Him should govern our relationship with others. For instance, I John 4:11 states:

"Beloved, if God so loved us, we also ought to love one another." (NASB)

Every time we offer genuine love, it is proof of the presence of God in us, a signature of creation by a God whose essence is love (I John 4:7-9).

The perpetual call and invitation for a relationship with Him is not only distinct but critical for every generation. Although God has provided the characteristics of being as a medium for relationship, and moral capacity, He does not force people into relationship with Him; He invites us.

God did not create humans as mere robots, or machines programed without having choice or will. If this were true, humans would be flawless, and sin would not have erupted in Eden, plunging the entire human race into condemnation. The cross and death of Christ would have been unnecessary, because man would be in perfect harmony with his Creator.

But He created humans with the capacity for intelligence, the ability and liberty to determine their own actions. However, because humans are finite in their abilities, the inclination to sin is ever present in the creature. Adam and Eve's actions in the Garden of Eden were determinants of their will, without direct power or influence by the Creator. As H. Christopher (1876) definitively notes, "The act of an intelligent being is the act of that being's will, which is self-determining..." [9]

When God gave humans, mental faculty to choose or decide upon a course of action, He licensed individuals as sovereign entities of their own behavior. The basic nature of will is its liberty and capacity to determine its own actions. This is one critical reason humans cannot and should not impose their will on another; or tell, order, or make one do or not do; Be or not Be. A man cannot tell a woman who to be, what she can or cannot do; conversely, a woman cannot dictate perquisites of manhood. Every individual is inherently free and can determine their own course of action. However, there is a dangerous caveat to that reality.

As an ongoing concession of the individual freedom God extends to humanity, He does not directly or arbitrarily leverage His power to impose His will on humans. As mentioned, He conversely invites us (upon accurate knowledge of Him) to synchronize our will with His. The Holy One does not force us to live right, He invites and encourages us into holy living, to praise and glorify Him by the same. God provides everything necessary for us to respond and experience this invitation successfully. For instance, II Peter 1: 3 notes:

> Seeing that His divine power has granted to us everything pertaining to life and godliness, through the true knowledge of Him who called us by His own glory and excellence. (NASB)

In Matthew 11:28-30, Jesus states:
Come to Me, all who are weary and heavy-laden, and I will give you rest. Take My yoke upon you and learn

from Me, for I am gentle and humble in heart, and YOU WILL FIND REST FOR YOUR SOULS. For My yoke is easy and My burden is light.

This is the great invitation for a significant exchange. It is a divine call into release, rest and reward, the efficacy of which is mediated through a covenant relationship with the Lord. God as Creator has provided the infrastructure for life and meaningful relationship with Him. There is an open invitation to enter His love, grace and to glorify Him as the Sovereign God of the universe. Ongoing worship, praise, spiritual union and fellowship, reverence, and living in His will are ideal markers of our relationship with God. This then becomes the teleological argument; the purpose for which every human exists, to glorify God (Is. 43:7; Col. 1:16; Rev. 4:11). Like the male, the woman's see the primary view of herself and her life through this lens and context.

3) Given the conclusion that the characteristics of being originate from the essence of God and are teleological (meaning they have divine purpose) then they must also be eternal. This realization underscores the indisputable fact that the plan of God includes a relationship with the creature far beyond the human experience, or our tenure on earth. As the woman grows to become and belong, she must do so understanding that her meaning and purpose are greater than herself and reach far beyond this world.

> The woman's right to choose is inherent, not be-
> cause she is a woman, but a created being to whom
> the Creator has commissioned will, within which is
> a sovereign capacity for self-determination.

But humans must tread cautiously and circumvent the temptation to making self-determination, access, and choice, life's
most coveted endgame. An exaggerated emphasis on these is
certain to leave God out of the picture. Life then loses its true
meaning and purpose, which, as noted, extends far beyond our
time on earth. The inevitable evolution of the woman must filter through a godly wisdom that notes not only her sovereignty
in, and significance to humanity, but divinity's undeniable interest in her in the afterlife. God's call and presence must
temper the woman's proverbial sojourn to exist meaningfully.
Except we make His call and presence the end game, we will
end up with a life that is meaningful only to us and our cheer-
leaders, but insignificant to the One we are most accountable.

Looking up, in the wake of raining glass from shattered ceilings,
the woman should not only see herself and her community, but
the Creator. For all that she is (her significance, aptitude,
strength, wisdom, grace, and voice) Divinity inspires and orchestrates. For a person to exist meaningfully then,
understanding the matrix and mission borne out of this human-
divine dynamic is of necessity.

The most powerful and treasured woman is the godly one living in complete awareness of her Creator and maximizing her inalienable gifts to produce an optimal life that not only elevates herself and impact community, but gives glory and praise to Him who authored her existence. The woman, a created specialty endowed with unique gifts from the Creator, enters the world with pre-assigned value and purpose that are irreducible, and designed to aid the heavenly agenda mitigated through the human experience. Toppling her male counterpart and claiming victory does not enhance her dignity, definition, importance, and responsibility. More truly, victory already lives in her. What is inevitably beneficial to the woman and her community is her awareness of and capacity to lean into the divine elements of her core self, step into the significance made for her, and simply be; and by being she will become; and becoming she will belong!

Hallmarks of womanhood are
undeniably notable both in
symmetry and dissimilarity.

One Octave

The Rock and Revolution of the Woman's Voice

everal years ago, Evelyn, a corporate attorney working for a major oil company based in the U.S., finds herself faced with ongoing challenges and unexpected bones of contention. As a Christian and a bi-racial female reared in a home with four siblings, she has had her share of navigating relational conflicts and jockeying for opportunity. There are three other exposures likely contributing to the perceptions and values that partially make her who she is today, namely the untimely death of her father on her seventh birthday, a devout mother, who taught her to always remain conscience of God; and an indelible encounter with an insolent person who did not see her as pretty during her adolescent period.

Having emerged from these, and refined by higher education later, she enters adulthood as a formidable God-fearing woman. But like some people, Evelyn wrestles with the boogiemen created by life's traumatic events.

For instance, although she is extremely attractive, confident, and proficient, the disrespectful comments leveled against her in the past consistently hunts her. Internal dialogue questioning whether her appearance is suitable saturates her mind daily. The absence of a father-figure to reaffirm her beauty and self-esteem exaggerates the issue.

Likely unknown to her, the revolving hair styles and excessive shopping are medicinal efforts to quail the discomfort emanating from the hole in her heart. Sometimes aches and pains irritate and infuriate their host, signs of which may not always be apparent. Shrouded in Evelyn's beauty and classiness is a mean-streak, or tendencies to anger, which likely rises from that indelible insult from her youth, and is protection, in her mind at least. When something irritates her, those beautiful eyes transform into a sharp look that will make a man's soul shutter. People closest to her describe her as the female version of her brother, who is a hot-headed muscleman, terrorizing and intimidating anyone on the wrong side of him. But unlike her brother, Evelyn's godly spirit, and the discipline usually developed in (but not limited to) professional people, helps her temper animated emotions arising from challenging circumstances, most of the time.

The way she mitigates her daily challenges in the corporate world is an exemplar of this. In an environment where male dominance too often unfolds in demeaning and sexist ways, navigating restrictions, denials, catcalls, and dodging ongoing lures into sexual relationships for corporate advancement, tax her days. Instead of raising her voice, wagging her finger, or stomping in protest, she takes a novel approach... an intellectual approach to mitigate daily challenges. Evelyn knows keenly that to effect changes in this environment requires one to assume power. Although outraged over some of their antics and tactics, she elects to speak out differently; she is selectively silent, yet she magnifies her voice. By consistently denying offers to engage unethical conduct for promotion, she speaks volumes about her godly character and integrity. In addition, Evelyn intimidates her male counterpart and opposition by remaining a consummate professional, with a no-non-sense approach to business. The caliber of her work is undeniably impressive, and always leaves the rest of the office, stunned. Her commitment to ethics and stellar performance always wins the day. It inevitably catapults her through doors of opportunity, which shatter glass ceilings, and elevate her into a position of power to make change.

But the daily dilemma at the office is not the only conundrum she has to tackle. There are those unexpected nightmares and conflicts also demanding attention and challenges her godly spirit and professional decorum. For instance, one weekend her son's minor league team takes a trip to a nearby city to take part in a round of playoffs. The team's coaches, players, and some of their family members hoard a bus for the trip.

Evelyn's husband (Larry) joins her and their son for the tournament. The six-hour drive gives space for loud chatter, laughter, and music. As the teams arrive in the city, their excitement grows. They can hardly wait to get off the bus, into their rooms and prepare for the activities ahead.

After settling in, the coaches meet with the team to review the agenda and schedule. In between scheduled practices, Larry takes a jog. But Evelyn elects to take a stroll just outside the motel, to keep an eye out for her son and the other teammates he is hanging out with. After walking around for about an hour, she takes a shortcut across the parking lot back to her room. Music playing loudly arouses her attention. She notices coaches sitting on the bus, joking around, and while listening to the music. As she moves past the bus, the pungent aroma of pot overwhelms her. Irritated, she beats on the door to gain access to the bus. As she enters, Evelyn finds that not only are they smoking pot, but drinking liquor as well. She is furious now, and the smoke and smell overtake attempts to say something. She quickly exits the bus and returns to her room to watch periodically from her window. Once the coaches emerge from the bus to begin practice, she barges out of her room to confront them for trying to manage the children while obviously high and intoxicated. One coach (Toby) did not appreciate Evelyn's approach, or the details of her complaint. With little regard for her femininity, he steps up into her face and animatedly argues. As their verbal gymnastics toggles back and forth, the commotion draws a crowd of players, parents, and other spectators.

The incident catches everyone by surprise. As they try to figure out what the conflict is about, the crowd mumbles, but
does not intervene. While the situation is quickly escalating,
Larry is returning from his jog. As he draws closer to the motel,
he hears the excitement, above which is the agitated, stressed,
and frantic sound of his wife's voice. His jog turns into a full
sprint. As he turns the corner into the parking lot, he sees Evelyn and the coach, toe-to-toe! More he sees Toby's finger is
pressing against her cheek as he screams an expletive and demands she get out of his face. Larry's surprise quickly converts
into anger, and his full sprint now becomes an offensive charge.
He yells out, "step away from her, or I will snap you in half!"
There was an immediate collective gasp from the crowd. The
stern warning even distracts Evelyn and coach Toby.

As Larry quickly approaches, one of the other coaches (Robert) realizes that he is heading for Toby steaming mad. Robert
springs into action now and intercepts him before he reaches
the coach. Grabbing him around his waist, Robert pulls him in
the opposite direction, while encouraging him to stay calm.
Meanwhile, Coach Toby feels belittled by the husband's warning and aggressive move and reactively charges in Larry's
direction. Other parents and coaches then react by grabbing
him and pulls him in the opposite direction as well. These
events happened quickly, and Evelyn did not realize that it was
her husband who issued the warning, and the person Robert is
restraining. Completely surprised, her hands cover her mouth
as she slowly moves toward Larry. She mumbles, what have I
done?

The reason Evelyn's husband's reaction surprises everyone is because Larry is usually as quiet as a mouse; people know him as professional, reserved, and friendly. In all the years of their marriage, even she has never witnessed what she saw in him that day. Evelyn becomes consumed with guilt. As she processes the turn of events, she thinks that her actions may have escalated the conflict.

When she walks up to her husband, he notices her hands slightly trembling. The event was obviously overwhelming for everyone. Larry calls for his son, and the three of them head back to their motel room. Seemingly still racked with guilt, Evelyn is unusually silent, which does not escape her husband's attention. He breaks the awkwardness by reassuring her. "You did the right thing... protecting children's environment and welfare is always the right thing to do... the issue was a legitimate bone of contention. Giving voice to ethics is what you do. It is okay. Your position is the right one." Teary eyed, Evelyn raises her head and slightly smiles. It was all she needed... a subtle reminder and a gentle nudge into the framework or ontology that makes her who she is. Tomorrow is game day. The family takes it easy the rest of the evening. As the day dawns, Evelyn rises, feeling much better about her decision to speak out about the coach's behaviors and the risk they posed.

As game time approaches, and everyone gathers for the event, there is an awkward undercurrent beneath the shouts and cheers for the players. Their son and the rest of the team were unsuccessful in their bid and lost the game. Evelyn and Larry decide to not take the trip back home with the team on the bus. They stay over an extra day to take in the local attractions, and then rent a car to drive back home. As they drove, Larry reassures Evelyn that she made the right move. Three weeks later, Evelyn appears before the commission that regulates little league football, coaches, staff, and volunteers. It was here that Evelyn draws from her legal mind and skills, and methodically and persuasively lay out her case. In typical fashion, Evelyn stuns the room, and effect change.

After hearing the complaint, the commission remove the coaches involved and enact regulation that prohibit the use of alcohol and drugs before or during game related activities. In addition, the commission make background checks and drug tests standard for coaches. Once again, the voice of the woman becomes revolution.

What is Voice?

Science has determined that the pitch of a woman's voice registering between 165 and 255 Hz, is naturally one octave higher than a man's registering between 85 to 155 Hz. [1] Her DNA prescribes that when she communicates, her voice is higher, softer, and often more melodious than her male counterpart. The beauty and delicacy of her voice is not testament of inferiority or weakness, but a tangible biological reminder she is a created specialty. The Creator's desire and intention that the female is distinct from her counterpart is clear. The woman's features, behavior, thought process, decision-making, and voice are more complex and far different from the male, yet God expects the man and the woman to live in one voice, in earthly union, and in spiritual harmony with Him, as a collective, and individual.

What exactly is voice? Its true meaning is multidimensional and reaches far beyond anatomical processes we normally associate with voice, i.e., air traveling through a windpipe and vibrating vocal cords. The voice obviously has a much more profound meaning and impact, which is clear by the voices of antiquity, and the contemporary clamor to speak and for people to hear. In this context, silence seems restrictive, controlling, with negative outcomes. However, this is not always the case.

The motivation, goal, and context decipher whether the demand for silence is discrimination, denigrating, or obstructive. But silence is not something we should fear. When employed strategically, it is influential. Having said this, do note, elevating silence as something consequential is not a hidden suggestion or attempt to silence the woman, but a concession that silence speaks, and sometimes, more powerfully. Given this, is the voice of the woman ever silent? Raising such a proposition does not dismiss or change awareness of targeted attempts (during antiquity and contemporary times) to control women by the overreaching application of God's mandates in communities of faith and in society.[2] Again, the emphasis is on the undeniable truth, that silence speaks powerfully.

I Peter 3:h notes that the woman's behavior alone can win over or change the heart of her unbelieving husband without saying a word. The accent is not on gender, nor designed as something prohibitive. The point of the text is that behavior is influential, it has voice. If we surmise that voice is audible in silence, or that a person's behavior speaks, and that the absence of a voice equates to the absence of an individual or group, what then is voice? One of the most fantastical revelations during this writing is the fact that the first time the word voice appears in humanity, is in Holy Scripture, and is interestingly about the woman. [3] When God began leveling consequences for disobeying rules, He inaugurates (which is in humanity's best interest) consequences for Adam's sin and failure; He says to him, "because you have listened to the voice of your wife and have eaten from the tree about which I commanded you, saying, 'You shall not eat from it'; cursed is the ground because of you ...". [4] Not that Eve was to be silent in this moment, and that Adam's error was allowing her to speak.

Adam's issue and sin is discoverable in the Hebrew word for "listen", which is Shama. In this text[5], the word describes one who gives in to, heed, or obey[6]. When the beautiful woman God gave him, spoke (likely) in a soft, yet efficacious way, rather than asserting leadership, and in effect, assume responsibility by protecting the woman from the voice of the Devil, he buckles, and chooses the voice of the woman over the command of God.

There are many other biblical facts and theological implications regarding the gullibility of Eve, the weakness of Adam, and the precise constitution of divine order. But the axis of this discussion is about the voice, its meaning and impact.

When extrapolating meaning from voice there are essential factors (a vocal nexus of sorts) one must consider. First, there must be a fundamental change from defining voice as sheer auditory production. We must see and herald voice as "vocal agency", that has material dimensions, within which are character, capacity, presence, language, and philological codes, that give body and order to spiritual, social, ancestral, and political principles. We must revere the voice as an ineffaceable force, and spatial orientation that has revolutionary tendencies. The right voice, spoken during crucial moments or contexts, can cause major changes.

The voice is an act of agency. Agency is a by-product of the inherent sovereignty given each person over their own determinations, or human will; it then is human capacity to advocate and affect how one operates in life and respond to the consequences or events emanating from their determinations.

Among the notable factors that give voice meaning and agency, material dimensions are likely paramount. Material usually refers to a special substance or a mixture of substances that make something what it is. Organically, material refers to the fabric of ones' being, the building blocks of the soul that make a person who they are.

They commonly extend across various sectors and contexts of life, which is what the phrase "material dimensions" means. Language is one component that forms these material dimensions. It is more than intelligible substance, but identity, capacity, and aspiration. American linguists Benjamin L. Whorf and Edward Sapir note that language shapes an individual's worldview and identity. [7] It is the rudiment and ferriage of the nucleus that unites the essentials of personhood; a snapshot of identity that is indelibly configured by the tenets of culture and the values rising out of them. Language expresses the sum of a person or being, which must include all internal dialogue and the desires horn out of these inner deliberations. As a host to one's inner-self, language is a carrier of philological (linguistic or language codes) spawned by cultural gatekeepers, beliefs, and religious rituals. It then serves as a communique, guide, and testament to an individual's perception, their status, and potential contribution to the circumstance and environment in which one find themselves.

In this context, philological codes are those things a person believes in, the communal, religious, and biblical rules they choose to accept, practice, and by which they identify and belong. In addition, language carries the aspirations of the heart, that which a person aims to be, become, and belong. It contains codes of being and desires that are reduced to words, signs, and symbols. For this reason, when people communicate through language, they usually select words carefully, at least with most people. Because the woman is usually aware of this, her words are often intentional, loaded, and persuasive.

The philological codes governing her will inform her language, as well as the style and emotion with which she elects to communicate. In fact, it is not uncommon for the woman to engage in "code switching" for survival. Code switching is a process used to switch from one language code to another when the context, circumstance, or environment demands it for survival.8 For instance, if a woman believes it is pertinent to her professional career or wellbeing, the codes governing her language in the home and community will change in the corporate world to those codified by that environment. She strategically speaks or will remain silent if she determines it is necessary in that moment. Sometimes, this may be good, but in others, not so. For example, if the woman's decision to remain silent is because of potential consequences for speaking truth to power (regardless if the power is real, or only perceived) may not be good for her, at least.

The takeaway is clear, during every moment of her existence, all that she is within and aspires to in life is manifest through language, her voice. Given this, how can humanity appreciate and care for the woman, if people wander from and are foreign to her inner-most dialogue expressed through her voice? When the godly woman speaks, her language carries all her experiences (both positive and negative) and includes her intelligence, wisdom, desire, spiritual paradigms; those maternal and matriarchal consults, and paternal sidebars influencing her unique perception, decision-making, and womanhood.

Capacity

The other aspect of material dimensions under discussion here is capacity. At face value, capacity refers to the ability to receive, hold or absorb, to perform or produce, to grow, develop or expand, and to have faculty. These configure the notion that language and concepts are as seeds. One of the most familiar examples of this truth presents in the Parable of the Sower, recorded in the Gospels: Matthew 13:1-23; Mark 4:1-20; Luke 8:4-15. These passages illustrate the Word of God as a type of seed that germinates when one receives by listening, accepting, and believing God's message. When the seed (Word of God) sprouts, it leads one into wisdom, obedience, and covenant relationship with God, through Christ, ultimately. The point is, when we receive the seed of the Word, it will grow, and growth brings change, maturity, and new opportunity.

This concept is likely clearer when revisiting the definition of the word seed and how it works. First, we technically defined a seed as the "fertilized, ripened ovule of a flowering plant containing an embryo, and capable normally of germination to produce a new plant broadly".[9] When conditions are ripe (oxygen, water, and temperature) the seed will germinate, which causes it to expand and ultimately reproduce the same substance and characteristics within it, producing change, in effect.[10] Because the material dimensions that create voice have within it language, it contributes to narratives, expand concepts, informs, educates, and foster performance, it inherently has capacity, and capacity either preserve or change.

Presence

Because voice is an act of agency, it is entity, subsistence, and life, through which one immanently has, and therefore entitled to a sense of presence. As previously noted, embedded in agency is the sovereign will of the individual, and one's ability to advocate the same. This point is critical to understanding the efficacy or value of having voice, especially regarding the woman. Because language codes (whether we communicate them orally or otherwise) and all that they represent, are inherent in the material dimensions of voice. To speak, to be heard, is to be present. In this context, presence is something that reaches far beyond physical representation. Vocal agency then creates presence, and gives access to executive boardrooms, committees, and classrooms; it allocates opportunity for conversation and contribution; and diminishes any spatial orientations[11] created by detractors and opposition.

In addition, voice automatically offers a "seat at the table", in the home and in the community. Although one's physical presence, inclusion and participation likely ensures advocacy, what is even more important is to speak, to be heard, whether directly, by inference, or influence. The woman is unique in this way, in that whether in the room she is present via her voice, and if present, then certainly a contributor and party of influence.

The Rock and Revolution of the Woman's Voice

When investigating acoustics, we learn that sound generates waves that "either stabilize or alter the surrounding environment." [12] The notion voice creates waves in multiple ways is an undeniable fact; and it certainly can stabilize or alter any environment. [13] The point that voice has material dimensions within it validates this notion. Silent voices manifest through behavior consistently show the ability to support or disrupt any environment, meaning it influences the tenor and tenet of any community.

History provides a panoramic view of notable women whose voice (whether via speech or behavior) either foraged continuity or caused revolution. *"Sawt* Al-Mar'a *Thawra",* an Arabic phrase that means the voice of the woman is revolution, is expedient here. [14] The world agrees that sound waves from the ineffaceable voices of prominent women of antiquity still pierce communities globally. National Geographic's (Nat-GEO) November 2019 edition[15] captures the spirited and efficacious power of women spanning the past century. Their exhaustive work and outstanding journalism are better respected by allowing it to stand as it is. For that reason, I find it unnecessary to duplicate their research by chronicling a list of women as examples of the stated fact.

Notwithstanding, National Geographic's edition give prominence to the voices and hearts of women jockeying to be heard in government, communities and trekking ever closer to gender equality. Slogans ranging from "We have the right to be heard" to "The future is female." They profile women, from the furthest recesses of antiquity to recent history and modern day as formidable warriors, fashion trail blazers, groundbreakers, media moguls, activists, peace makers and politicians.

Nat-GEO index the woman's rise, contribution, and revolution across various professional disciplines, such as physics, medicine, education, military, and business. Besides these, is the woman's notable rise to the office of the vice presidency of the United States of America. Nat-GEO present women as forces disrupting the "status quo", like the Defiant Sisters (Nuns) of India, and the fiery protest of the women of New Delhi, who demanded from their government the right to be safe from rape.[16]From every corner of the globe, society experiences the woman's voice as a rock and revolution.

The best course to capture the magnitude of the revolutionary feature of the woman's voice is to draw parallels between her voice and the words "rock and revolution" as defined in geological contexts. Revolution usually refers to a "sudden or momentous change in a situation." In geology, revolution is "a time of major crustal deformation when folds and faults form."[17] I use this parallel because it showcases the woman's strength and modulation during intense challenge or pressure, and its aftermath. Geology suggests folds show "twists and bends of rocks" caused by constant compression[18,] and faults are cracks in the earth's crust generated by tectonic move-ment.[19]

For pressure, stress, and movement to lead to folds and faults, the material of the rock must transform under heat and pressure, without extending beyond capacity. [20] In this context, "deform" means to alter the original state or size of rock mass, especially by folding or faulting. Can you not see it? How many narratives of old and contemporary tales of the woman's challenges and victories do we know and witness? She is unique when under pressure; and like the rock, she modulates, and rises to meet whatever challenge or call; proving in effect that which compresses, oppresses, denies, and rejects transforms into building blocks for her to rise, kindling for her to blaze, and provocation for her to move. It breeds life into the adage, "that which does not destroy, strengthens." When a woman is folding and faulting in response to antics and pressure imposed on her, by either her environment or life circumstances, what one is witnessing is involuntary processes of modulation, geared toward her survival and headway.

Remember, the woman is a "created specialty" and when under duress or challenge, the information code in her DNA programs her to draw from the flexibility, strength, and wisdom embedded within. Like special rocks that create folds and faults during unique geological events, the woman transforms under the heat and pressure of her circumstance. When life deals powerful blows, she will reel; when it crushes her, she will reassemble; when she breaks, she will mend; when life denies her, she will give herself permission; bury her, and she will dig her way out; try losing her in life's jungle, she will find her way home. The woman is a natural survivor.

The Creator has ordained the woman as the medium through which life continues and the primary source that nurtures, whether this manifests biologically, or by nurturing and loving others to whom she did not give birth. Irrespective of the context, her capacity to love and nurture is innate. Because of this, the divine order for her to not only live, but function optimally is irrevocable. As noted, the woman is an indispensable human being. She will always survive. Why is this important? When the woman speaks, the bedrock and material dimensions of her voice carry essentials for survival.

The voice of the woman usually leans toward support for the greater good. Her capacity to nurture and love extends beyond her own to include her community and society-at-large. Her voice then often alters traditional surfaces and contexts to include fairness, equality, and opportunity, enabling and contributing to the health and wellness of humanity. Like a rock, she stabilizes. The woman's natural spirit, which is persistent, strong, focused and undeniably impactful, is in her voice; if when she speaks, it often disrupts the "status quo" by breaking through traditional frameworks and contexts that are too often poised against her rise, her very being.

Not that all things traditional are wrong, and that all changes are good. Irrespective of the rightness or wrongness of tradition and change, what is noteworthy is that the woman has a voice. When the woman's voice coalesces it usually spawns permanent revolution. When she raises her voice, her character, capacity, presence, and power are notably apparent.

We must not ignore its influence and impact, but respect it. There is value in the voice of a woman. All we need is to look back into history to see and know that most of the revolutions spawned by the voice of the woman are changes that contribute to the progress and health of individuals, families, and communities. We are better served as a society, when medians for the woman's voice are not only readily available but appreciated. Her voice is just as vital as her being. In fact, her voice is who she has become. Notwithstanding, the woman must remember she too is a created being and must therefore always seek to honor and glorify God through her voice. It is through her divinely appointed gifts, talents, and capacity that she rocks and revolutionizes life.

*Humility, grace and dignity are
meaningful exhibits of her beauty.*

Visions of a Woman
The Mural, Mirror, and Magnifier

*W*hen the Creator gave the woman sight, her beautiful eyes not only process color differently, and have much greater peripheral vision than the man, but connect to a brain exceptionally different. Her vision (which is not limited to her physical eyes, but her mind's eye and heart) usually has a comprehensive view of life.

There are several approaches to defining the word vision. The usual depiction of a woman's vision highlights her foresight, that ability to perceive the significance of events or contexts and prepare for them in advance. Like the loving mother of Lemuel, King of Massa, who penned the noted passage of Proverbs 31: 1-9, within which the motherly advice foresees her son's rise to power, and potential pitfalls and dangers from excessive alcohol and unprincipled women. The instructions include behavior for governance. Queen Esther is another vivid example of a woman's vision. Upon learning about a scheme to destroy her people, she had intelligent foresight to plan and help divert her community from genocide. [1]

WOMAN: BEAUTY - POWER- DIVINITY
IN MOTION

But in this chapter, vision is not only intelligent foresight, but shows the way one sees, or conceives something; situational discernment, a mental masterpiece created by communal experience and imagination. This chapter gleans and makes prominent some of the schematic ideas contributing to the woman's vision or worldview, their divine baseline, and how the human experience affects the tendencies and characteristics of these. This impact presents uniquely in this chapter as a mural (the woman's public view) a mirror (the woman's personal view) and a magnifier (the woman's protective view). The concepts regarding visions of a woman (as presented here) are merely an inaugural to a more complex, multiphasic discussion; and is certainly not how every woman describes the building blocks of her vision or worldview.

Irrespective of the characteristics indigenous to the woman's vision, many women likely see the principles and wisdom codifying their worldview as something unique to others. Each woman then brings a distinct perspective to society.

The Mural

On a sizzling Saturday in Phoenix, Arizona, Aiyana, an 18-year-old Native American (known by her community as "A-y-2") sits in the window stool of her high-rise residence. Drowning in boredom, she watches heatwaves dance up from the hot parking lot below. "A-y-2" moved to Phoenix 18 months ago to live with her grandmother, after relationship with her parents fractured. Although not gay, her "tomboyish" style often limits the number of friends and associates with whom she connects, forcing her into solitary more often than she prefers.

As she looks out beyond the rising heat, her attention shifts to a massive wall of an office building in the distance, which is fertile territory in her mind. Because A-y-2 is a muralist, a surface such as the one she sees is prime real estate for her next mural project, or artistic expression. She quickly gulps the last two drops of water, grabs two additional bottles, her cell phone, and throws them into her backpack, which already contains multiple cans of spray paint. Sprinting down the stairs, she yells out to her grandmother, "I will be back later!" Her grandmother responds, "where are you going? It is 108 degrees outside!" As she closes the door behind her, A-y-2 replies in a fading voice, "I have my phone!" Relieved over breaking out her suffocating boredom, and excited about another opportunity to paint, she jumps on her scooter in route to the office building.

While approaching the building, her mind is in deep thought about what she would like to paint. She parks the scooter on the sidewalk, and then suddenly realizes that it is Saturday, and no one is likely in the building to give permission to paint. Bummed over the fact no one is in the building; she squats against the building with her face in her hands. But the urge to paint and express herself is too great... she reaches into her backpack and pulls out her spray paint... stares at the cans for few seconds... she looks around and notices there is not much traffic on Saturday. She goes for it! As the hissing sound of spray cans echoed between the buildings, vibrant colors erupt and artfully stain the side of the building. As she paints, A-y-2 believes the owner or manager will fall in love with her painting, and not complain at all. She confidently begins her mural project. It was a mural capturing her vision of freedom, friendship, and community.

A mural refers to a painting that applies to or made as a component of the surface of a wall or ceiling. [2] It drafts, captures, and incorporates architectural elements of the surface and its surrounding into the painting. The adage that a picture is a thousand words, is an appropriate notion for murals, in that one of the silent objectives of them is to create a dialogue about a topic (i.e., social, cultural, economic, etc.); and it often reflects current affairs.

It then enhances community, and free speech, because it creates a palpable place or destination. The efficiency of murals is a common theme across various locations. Visit Hotel Lisboa in Mexico City, you will discover a giant mural of La Catrina, the iconic Lady Death. Roll up to the intersection of 4th and Merrick in Los Angeles, California, a mural of a couple positioned head-to-head in an expression of love will capture your attention. If you travel to the Mile-High-City (Denver, Colorado) you will find murals of George Floyd, Elijah McClain, and Atatiana Jefferson, indelible images of victims of hate and brutality in this modern day. A stop in Philadelphia, which is of course the mural capital of the world, will uncover their "Maskup Philadelphia" mural, which highlights the persistent danger and drudgery of the COVID-19 Pandemic. The distinguishing hallmarks of murals (which are freedom of expression, strategic dialogue, creative-placemaking, community building and reflection) are important parts of the woman's worldview, which is illustrated by her decision-making and agency. Among these, freedom of expression is chief. The woman's need to express herself is innate. [1] Freedom of expression affords an individual the right to one's own opinion across various contexts. The mural gives the artist venue to capture and express his or her sentiment about life.

Depicting the woman's vision as a mural, speaks to her assimilation and embodiment of her community's voice, and its condition, especially when that condition reflects concerns that are critical to her own aspirations, and the humanity of others. Whether these are social injustices, education deficiencies, healthcare, creating access to equality and opportunity, or foraging paths to success, she showcases these as she sees or understands their affects.

In the same way the mural becomes a component of its surface and incorporates the elements and surroundings of the environment, the woman organically connects to her community. Her natural caring spirit intricately embeds challenges and concerns of the community into her thought process and vision. Looking out into her world then, she sees her community kaleidoscopically, as a destination to which she belongs, and with which she seeks harmony.

The goal is not simply harmonizing just to exist, but to contribute valuably to any resolutions effecting her community's most urgent needs. This push not only simultaneously construct identity but commends her as a critical partner in developing communal wellness. Her participation in the community's life as a volunteer for the local Food Bank, the church's Saturday clothing give-a-way, a member of the Montessori school's parent advisory committee, or heading up after-school programs for girls, extends her personal convictions regarding the needs of the community.

The woman's innate drive to express (in this case) sentiments regarding community needs and goals sets up the next important composite and hallmark of a mural, strategic dialogue. She strategically engages stakeholders regarding critical concerns requiring proper representation, calculated focus, and productivity from knowledge, expertise, and effective policies. Dialogue about issues of concern is something the woman does well. Her voice signals what she sees.

When her vision functions as a mural in this context, it becomes motivation for inviting others to discuss the issues and to take part in the resolution. This often causes the woman to become a "creative- place maker", which is another important aspect of her vision as a mural. Creative-placemaking usually refers to the collaborative efforts of artists, art specific organizations, and community development leaders to fuse art and culture into community revitalization. [4] Notwithstanding, in this chapter it refers to engaging community residents in processes necessary for community development.

As a creative-place maker, the woman is visible in committees, boards, neighborhood association meetings, book clubs and protests. These are venues and mediums through which she champions the clarion call to action around a cause or community challenge. She looks for opportunities to hold strategic dialogue, and when they are not readily available, she creates them, ensuring that stakeholders address the community's cause or challenge. Her aim is simple, to encourage community building and reflection, which are also critical aspects of a mural. Appreciation of community building requires a basic understanding of the word community, at minimum. Community, in its simplest form, refers to the alignment of people and groups of varying backgrounds and characteristics, who connect via social ties, common perspectives, and work together in a particular area or location.

Community building then, carries the idea of enhancing relationships, commonality, and a collective investment into the wellness of groups. As she surveys her community, she is attentive to doors and bridges that lead to opportunity. Sometimes, her stance and involvement in the community will "trouble knowledge" in ways that challenge the status-quo, which has its pros and cons within itself. But her singular focus in this context is to bring people together to improve standards and wellbeing, to build community in effect.

The Mirror

"Mirror, mirror on the wall, who is the fairest of them all?" [5] A familiar line quoted through the decades by young girls and women alike. It is a misquote of a red-letter line in the 1937 film, Snow White, and the Seven Dwarfs. The original line says, "Magic mirror on the wall...". [6] Regardless, it is the misquote that popularizes and captures the hearts of little girls around the world. They stand in front of pink framed mirrors and vanity sets in quest for affirmation of beauty. Reflections displayed by mirrors are undeniably impartial, in that it will only exhibit the exact image in front of it. We believe the people of Anatolia (which is Turkey today) invented mirrors approximately 8,000 years ago, by polishing volcanic rock.[7] Historians also believe that the Babylonians and the Egyptians used polished copper for mirrors during 4,000 and 3,000 BC, respectively.

In 1835 the German chemist, Justus Von Liebig perfected the
method for making mirrors, by applying a layer of metallic silver to the back pane of the glass.[8] This would later become the
template for mass production. A sophisticated process that
places the vacuum accumulation of aluminum or silver onto the
glass substrate is how mirror manufactures make them today.
We use mirrors in different ways for various reasons. Take a
trip to the local gym, you will find mirrors inundated throughout the workout space. Mirrors are excellent aids in training.
We sometimes use them as security, theft detection in grocery
and department stores. What is notable about mirrors is that
we design them to reveal things in real time. Unlike fairytales,
mirrors cannot show the future or a snapshot from the past.

What you see in that moment is the real deal, one's current
state. Scientists also employed mirrors to measure self-recogni-
tion in humans and animals. The Scripture also uses the
concept of a mirror as an important tool for spiritual reflection
and development. For instance, in chapter one of the New Testament book of James, lies a passage familiar to many analytical
students of Scripture. Here the writer depicts the Word of God
as a mirror.

> But prove yourselves doers of the word, and not merely
> hearers who delude themselves. For if anyone is a hearer of
> the word and not a doer, he is like a man who looks at his
> natural face in a mirror. For once he has looked at himself
> and gone away, he has immediately forgotten what kind of

person he was. But one who looks intently at the perfect
law of liberty, and abides by it, not having become a forget-
ful hearer but an effectual doer, this man will be blessed in
what he does. James 1:22-25 NASB

Two of the important keys found in this passage are the Greek
words used for the word "<u>looks</u>". Is first usage in the passage,
"<u>looks</u> at his natural face..." the Greek word is katanoeō, which
means to perceive, observe carefully.[9] Thayer's Greek-English
Lexicon of the New Testament, adds that the word means to
"consider attentively" to fix one's mind upon something to understand it.[10] But the second time the word "looks" appears in
the passage, "But one who <u>looks</u> intently..." a different Greek
word is in play, i.e., parakuptō and refers to stooping down or
looking into for a closer look;[11] it means to lean into in order to
"see something exactly";[12] to recognize it for what it is, and for
one to bend over the mirror to examine more minutely. Thayer
suggests the word means to stoop to "look carefully into, in-
spect curiously", so one would become acquainted with
something.[13]

In every illustration regarding mirrors, we expect the beholder
to see themselves as presented in their reflection. At that moment, it calls the beholder to note the details displaying in front
of them. Mirrors have messages. But when I talk about the mirror as one aspect of a woman's vision, I am not referring to the
reflection she experiences from a direct gaze into a mirror, but
the reflection of herself through the gaze or eyes of others.

This is the "mirror effect". 14 It is what I also call 'perspective probing' which is an instinctive critical analysis of the interrelation of people and their circumstances, with one's self-image, and their comparative significance. The woman's looking glass then surveys her community, environment, and personal perspectives in a triangulated way.

This process not only makes her capable of decoding the indelible identity and value of others (which is palpable through their circumstance) but readily sharpens her own identity, perspective and calling. It summons her into action, which is clear by the woman's compassion and creativity in response to her visual analysis and understanding of community challenges. This helps her not only identify problems but assume a vital role in the solution. Given the way her vision forms, she usually can speak about issues and their solutions in an inform way. We must then invite woman to the table as a relevant stakeholder in the overall health of the community.

Remember the hired shearer in chapter two, who approaches Abigail about the impending threat and doom to the community, caused by her wayward husband. As noted, turning to Abigail is testament of her ability to see the situation from a broad view and offer a tenable solution in its wake. The solution she offers is born out of the triangulation of the people involved, the extenuating circumstances and who she is at heart. The narrative is a classic example of a woman beholding her reflection through the eyes of others.

The Magnifier

The other important aspect of the woman's vision is its function as a magnifying glass. Technically, as an object, a magnifying glass is a "system of optical components that magnifies." It enlarges its target. A magnifier can also be a person who lifts awareness by focusing light or calling attention to a thing or situation. The woman's visual acuity detects and lock in on concerns that have a broad impact on her community. It is an alarm system of sorts that signals leadership, gatekeepers, and constituents into action, either in honor of God or defense of humanity and the greater good. Her inalienable broad view of things not only detects negative outcomes, but certainly contributes to innovation across multiple disciplines and sectors of life.

Given her created role, she has visionary skill-sets that compliments what God has called her into. When the Creator gave sight and vision to the woman, He uniquely equips her for capacity to love, support, and contribute, protect, and enlarge the efficacy of community and humanity broadly. The woman who can see her reflection in the eyes of her Creator is one of immense beauty and power, and is an invaluable treasure to her community, in fact, life itself. The virtuous woman detailed in Proverbs 31:10-31 is the ivory tower of godly women. The life of such a woman is a meaningful display of grace and divinity positively affecting all benefactors of her God-given treasures. Her beauty and contributions to humanity are undeniable.

One inherent property of a woman's beauty is discoverable through her unique complexity.

Properties of a Woman's Beauty

"He has made everything beautiful in its time..."
-Eccl. 3:11

he aesthetic[1] argument heralds that the mere existence of beauty shows a higher standard through which it originates. It oscillates between the subjective view ("beauty is in the eye of the beholder") and objective beauty (which refers to its actual existence or reality). In addition, is the debate about whether our awareness of beauty is intrinsic. Definitively, in theological contexts aesthetics falls within the "design argument"[2] and refers to the study of beauty, taste, architecture of which the Creator God is its sole designer and origin, and the best explanation for it. If we surmise that the God of Heaven is the Creator (and we must[3]) then we also conclude that He has a predilection for beautiful things, which is not only clear through beautiful people, but the universe's testimony of naturally stunning architecture and raw materials.

For instance, the diamond (the woman's best friend, as we claim it) forms at a depth that pierces the earth's mantle, where the pressure and temperature are mesmerizing. This immense heat and tension cause carbon atoms to bond and coagulate in a way that create crystals. Experts believe a one-carat diamond to contain billions of carbon atoms that are immobilized, which produces a crystalline structure of fire and brilliance.[4] As the diamond dazzles and dances on the woman's hands, ears, or neck, it creates an effect called "scintillation"[5], the dramatic impact from a real precious stone, an outcome to which we have grown accustomed. The ruby, which is also formed in an environment like the diamond, is another spectacular measure of divine artistry. Formed from corundum, a mineral super packed with aluminum and oxygen atoms, it produces a deep red appearance when small amounts of chromium integrate. When this same environment integrates with traces of titanium and iron, it creates the exquisite blue sapphire we all know.[6]

Precious stones are not the only signature of God's interest in beauty. One only need to look up into the night sky to behold the impressive constellation of stars, or survey images from the Hobble telescope, which has sent back jaw dropping images of galaxies and other remarkable celestial events. The bible is correct, when it states, "The heavens are telling of the glory of God; And their expanse is declaring the work of His hands."[7]

In addition, are those beautiful places in the world obviously designed by the Creator. The Great Barrier Reef and White Haven Beach of Australia, and Angel Falls of Venezuela, which cascades 3,213 feet down in Canaima National Park, or the stunning blue waters surrounding the islands of Fiji, are powerful examples. The Creator God has 'a thing' for beauty. Even when God gave instructions for making priestly garments, He mentions beauty as one aim for the garment.[8] That divine architecture is impressively beautiful makes complete sense, for the Lord is beautiful.[9] The chief composite of the Lord's beauty is His holiness, because holiness is beautiful.[10] Aesthetics then points to God as its reason for being, which includes a teleological perspective. Again, teleological refers to "divine purpose", that yields perfect results. If beauty originates and exists because of God, it then has an aim or rationale defined entirely by Him. Everything God creates, and everything He does, reflects Him. His actions and creation are worthy of praise.

This answers whether our awareness and appreciation of beauty is innate. Research suggests that humans prefer beautiful faces during early infancy.[11] Everything the Lord does is resolute, driven solely by His will[12]. Regardless of our ability to comprehend what He is doing; He does nothing without cause or purpose. Those aspects of His will requiring or summonsing His creatures to respond are: 1) communicated and directed by the Creator[13]; 2) secured by His providence mediated through His people,[14] which sometimes He enacts through His communicable attributes. For example, God requires those in relationship with Him to be holy. "You shall be holy, for I am holy."[15] In fact, we cannot enter His presence without being holy. The consequence of entering God's presence unprepared is death instantly.[16] But it is impossible for any human to rise to the level of holiness necessary for not only relationship with God, but to enter His presence. We find the remedy for this conundrum in God's communicable attributes. Through the death of Christ and the indwelling presence of His Spirit, God makes us holy enough to commune with Him. He will always provide a medium for that which He demands of His creation.

Given this natural modus operandi, humans then have an intrinsic awareness and response to beauty, the goal of which is to glorify Him as Creator. For instance, when Adam sees Eve for the first time, it obviously enthralled him with joy. His soul flips with excitement, which is not captured in the translation from Hebrew to English. We know that the grammatic structure of the Hebrew text of Genesis 2:23 suggests that Adam launched into a song of sorts, or poetry when he laid eyes on Eve. But how did Adam know to respond to Eve in that way? Whatever he determined good about Eve, how did he know it was good? As noted, it is highly likely that Eve was stunning, in ways and to a degree the current world has never seen. Remember, God creates her during a period in which the fallenness of man is unrealized. Although short-lived, Eve is free of any deterioration. She is flawless!

Freshly created himself, it must be that Adam has within him the capacity to discern and appreciate beauty, which I believe is a basic instinct. Appreciation of beauty in the animal kingdom is also recognizable. The peacock spreads its tail to showcase beautiful feathers, and Frigate bird of the Galapagos Islands will inflate his red throat pouch to attract. "God has made everything beautiful in its time...".[17]

What is Beauty?

People commonly use the word beauty to describe a beautiful woman.[18] What then are the properties of a woman's beauty? Even if we surmise that beauty is in the "eye of the beholder", still, what makes her beautiful? How is it measured and with what? Does the length and texture of her hair play a role in that assessment? What about the color of her eyes, shape of her brow, the length of her eyelashes, or how thin her lips are? Will the fact that her face strategically sinks inward or fills out matter? Is this beauty notable by the strength of her walk or a gentle sway? Do high-heels, tight jeans, mascara, and a soothing voice factor? Is beauty physical at all? To explore the answer to these, consider two critical terms in the chapter title; "Properties" and then "beauty", as we use it in historical and contemporary contexts. Properties (as used in this chapter) refer to unique characteristics or beneficial qualities and power belonging to the woman. Second, is the word beauty, which has an interesting etymology.

The first usage of the word is not apparent to most, because the text uses it during God's stamp of approval on His creative brilliance, i.e.,

> Then God said, Let there be light; and there was light. God saw that the light was <u>good</u>... Genesis 1:3-4 NASB.

The Hebrew root for the word good (Towb) is the same as the word used for beauty (Tôwb)[19] which immediately suggests that "good" is an inherent aspect of beauty. The first-time the word beauty describes women occurs in Genesis 6:2,

> ...that the sons of God saw the daughters of men were beautiful, and they took wives for themselves, whomever they chose. NASB.

The Hebrew definition of beauty expands to include the concept of excellence, delight, something precious, moral goodness and aesthetics. In Genesis 29:17, the text describes Rachel as "beautiful". But the word used to describe Rachel differs from the word noted above. Here the word is Tiph'ereth, which shows characteristics that enhance, in this case, that which enhanced Rachel's appearance, her visual equity and impact.[20] Although the word beauty or beautiful can describe one's physical appearance today, the components that give definition to the terms reach beneath the surface of the individual to a much more qualitative essence. The Greek noun for beauty, καλλοσ (kallos) as a verb (καλεω) means "to call". It suggests that beauty is an object of appetite or desire, in the sense that the aim is to achieve that which is good, to make or experience beauty. As noted, this was God's aim (in part) in the world's creation and of man, to present something good or beautiful, because He is Himself the standard by which we measure anything good or beautiful. This stresses the fact that good is an inherent quality or component of beauty. Thomas Aquinas (1225-1274) was an Italian philosopher, respected as the greatest Scholastic philosopher. He chronicled a comprehensive synthesis of Christian theology, in which he notes three essential qualities of beauty (truth, beauty, and goodness). Ironically, Aquinas points out that good and beauty are the same, as each of them produces form.[21]

The Rearview

But through the progression of time and revolving cultural values, the standards measuring beauty changed. For instance, the word beauty or beautiful developed as something tangible, and that stoke human senses. In Vulgar Latin, beauty was a state of being pleasing to the senses, something fine. During the early 14th century, the Anglo-French word for beauty meant physical attractiveness.[22] By the late 14th century the phrase "beautiful woman" is first recorded in English and used more commonly in its wake. The 14th century's meaning and application shift to incorporate concepts of pleasure and emotion for beauty. In the mid-15th century, beautiful meant anything pleasing to the eye, ear, mind, or soul.

In 1756, beautiful became that which possessed beauty. As time progresses, the phrase "beautiful people" came to mean the "fashionable set" and was first used in Vogue Magazine in 1964. As pleasure-seeking people emerged around the world, beauty became more associated with what pleased the beholder. One source defined beauty as,

> *"the quality present in a thing or person, that gives intense pleasure, or deep satisfaction to the mind, whether arising from sensor manifestation (as shape, color, sound etc.) a meaningful design or pattern or something else..."*[23]

One part of Merriam-Webster's Dictionary's definition of beauty states,

> *"...aggregate of qualities in a person that pleasurably exalt the mind or spirit..."*

Pleasure has emerged as a common facet in the concept of beauty. This notion and reality give substance to the idea of aesthetic hedonism, which suggests there is a necessary connection between beauty and pleasure; and that for one to experience beauty, there must be a pleasurable benefit for the beholder.[24] Writing about beauty in the Oxford Companion to Philosophy, Ted Honderich notes Thomas Aquinas' position, which postulates that beauty is "that which pleases in the apprehension of it."[25]

Some researchers have noted the waist-hip-ratio[26] as an important marker of beauty.[27] However, women rarely prefer their bodies used as a marker for beauty and value.

Most times, beauty is inherent to culture, or what influences it in part. What then is beautiful in one culture may differ from another one. How we communicate beauty also bares significance. For instance, the historical portrayal of white women in movies, tv shows and advertisement contributed to the erroneous perception of an Eurocentric standard of beauty, which conceived the notion women of color were inferior, subsequently. The "black is beautiful" movement emerged in the 1960s as a protest to this kind of thinking.[28]

There have been positive and negative outcomes from so much emphasis on beauty throughout time, especially in the 21st century. For instance, one study suggests that students considered exceptionally beautiful score higher grades than those whom others view as less beautiful, or common.[29] Beautiful people are more likely seen as truthful or honest, even if they are not. In the book Psychology and Law: Truthfulness, Accuracy and Credibility, is a study simulating criminal trials of defendants who were beautiful. The study reveals that most of the beautiful defendants were less likely to be convicted, and those who were received light or minimum sentences for their crimes.

Notwithstanding, the study showed beautiful defendants were more likely convicted of crimes involving swindling, which suggests that jurors believed beauty played a role in this kind of offense.[30] If you look closely, you will see this dynamic in play across sectors throughout societies. News channels featuring women as anchors or meteorologists host attractive women, which is sure to improve viewership. Beauty also has a monetary impact, so much so, CNN | Time Warner Cable, raised the question, "Do pretty people earn more?"[31] When applying for credit or for a loan, people who are less attractive are less likely to be approved. This type of mindset and behavior is lookism, discriminatory practices that are based solely on one's appearance.[32] Given cultural conditioning, lookism has emerged as a pattern of behavior that so many have unwittingly adapted. Discrimination (whether in favor or against the woman) is a practice God dislikes.[33] The true properties of a woman's beauty then, must include more than what lies in the eye of the beholder.

The Beauty of the Lord

Before detailing the properties of a woman's beauty, one truth that bares mentioning, and that gives identity and vitality to these assets, is the beauty of the Lord. The beauty of the Lord is the canvas that configures, coalesces, and animates the properties of the woman's beauty. The notion that the Lord is beautiful is likely foreign to the average person's mind, because most people usually associate God with love and goodness, but not beauty necessarily. Second, people's perception of beauty is more sensual than spiritual; and the third reason this concept is likely alien to most is because no human has ever seen God in all His holiness and glory.[34] God is a spirit,[35] therefore invisible.[36] The human eye cannot see anything supernatural.[37] When the bible details direct human and divine encounters, such as Moses' encounter with God, God presents in an altered or adjusted form to prevent instant death.[38] Again, no human can see Him in His Fullness or unadjusted state and live to talk about it. Although the Lord discloses Himself, the absence of familiar tangible evidence makes it difficult for humans to assign beauty or beautiful as a critical composite of the Lord's splendor.

Notwithstanding, Scripture declares His beauty, and as mentioned, He then is the origin of beauty. But how is He beautiful? When contemplating or discussing the beauty of the Lord, that He is beautiful in a manner and measure defined by Him alone is noteworthy. There is no greater standard that can measure Him. No instrument or assessment can either confirm or deny His inherent status of beauty. We can only know what He discloses of Himself within the Canon of Scripture. From this we know that His glory is so magnificent it produces radiance brighter than anything known to man. Putting this in perspective, the Apostle Paul notes that God "dwells in unapproachable light...".[39]

This light is not the totality of His being. He is not the light, but dwells in it. This light emitting from His essence acts as a cover or coat that covers Him. The Psalmist captures it beautifully:

> Bless the Lord, O my soul! O Lord my God, You are very great; You are clothed with splendor and majesty, covering Yourself with light as with a cloak, …
> Psalm 104:1-2 NASB.

The immensity and intensity of this light is such that it cannot be subdued or overcome, much less penetrated to see the Holy One in totality, hence He is "unapproachable". Intense fire and light reflect the beauty and holiness of God's presence. In Deuteronomy 4:24 and Hebrews 12:29, describes God as a "consuming fire." In addition, during their first meeting, the Lord presents Himself to Moses as a burning bush.[40] Exodus 19:18-25 notes that historic and astonishing event in which the Lord descends on Mt. Sinai. God fills the top of the mountain with fire, and like a fiery furnace the smoke billowed upward as the mountain shook violently at the presence of the Lord. It was a beautiful yet terrifying experience for the people congregated at the base of the mountain. Paul's unforgettable moment of conversion happens when he meets the Lord while traveling to Damascus. The Lord presented Himself as an intense light that blinds Paul for three days afterwards.[41] Even with these instances available, you may still ask or wonder, if He is invisible, how then is He beautiful?

From one angle, we can easily point to Christ, who is the manifestation of God in the flesh. Christ is God, and God is Christ.[42] He is the exact representation of God,[43] which is why Christ says, "He who has seen Me, has seen the Father."[44] However, even as the "radiance of His glory and exact representation of His nature" Christ is made in a way that was unappealing to humans. Isaiah 52:14 and 53:2,3 portray the Christ as one without stately splendor:

> Just as many were astonished at you, My people, So His appearance was marred more than any man, and His form more than the sons of men. Is. 52:14 NASB.

> For He grew up before Him like a tender shoot, and like a root out of parched ground; He has no stately form or majesty that we should look upon Him, nor appearance that we should be attracted to Him. Is. 53:2.

The Savior was not the stunning fair skin, blonde hair, blue-eyed treasure on two feet, nor dark chocolate thunder with wavy hair and a muscular physique, often conceived by modern artists. Dr. Joan Taylor rightfully notes in her book, Jesus did not look like any of the contemporary images portraying him.[45] Although seemingly extremely unattractive, as the "exact representation of God" He was beautiful then and is now. How is this so?

The best explanation is because we cannot define the beauty of the Lord as a godly corporal phenomenon, or a quantifiable inanimate object of sorts. It is not something framed or characterized by the human's conditioned perception of beauty. His beauty exists independent of any external influence, which He alone governs. It is self-sustained, immeasurable, and eternal. The beauty of the Lord is a paradoxical matrix, in that He is naturally invisible, yet His beauty is clear before the entire universe.

The beauty of the Lord is visible through His eternal attributes, which are magnificently displayed and awesomely experienced. Although too grand and complexed for the human mind and senses, it tantalizes men into its reality. His attributes, holiness, love, justice, mercy, truthfulness, jealousy, omnipotence, wrath, wisdom, omniscience, omnipresence, goodness, independence, and eternity are not a list of characteristics pointing to some part of Him but are in fact His Being. He is all these simultaneously, perfectly, and eternally. Because of the perfection of these attributes in Him, they spawn splendor and majesty unparalleled to anything that exists. Their collected essence showcases the immutable properties of beauty.

Constructing the beauty of the Lord as a canvas then suggests that the critical components that comprise the properties of beauty are not only unknowable, but nonexistent independent of Him; and that His essence is the foundation of true beauty.

In art, a canvas help generate visual effects that inoculate or bind lines, colors, and shapes to produce form, clarity, balance and meaning. In like manner, the beauty of the Lord ushers life into the characteristics of beautiful things. In the same way a white background makes colorful lines, shapes, and images pop. This then exposes a truth that is not clear to most, except for God Himself. Authentic beauty is not the work of the one who holds it but derives out of something freely given.[46] This notion channels the proper way in which we must view and interpret beauty.

Humans must always assess and process beauty through the prism of the Holy Creator. Conceptualizing beauty merely through the imperfect and unimaginative scopes of human wisdom will only subjugate beauty to the fallenness of man. Beauty constructed in this context becomes diluted and dishonored by feeble attempts to add value through barren, fleeting and inconsequential tenets humans conventionally ascribe to it. One example of this is in Isaiah 3: 16- 26, in which God pronounces judgment against the women of Judah, whose attitude toward beauty cause them to spiral into moral decay, dishonoring God in effect. They had become beautiful for the sake of beauty, and had become proud, arrogant, and self-serving. God gives a stinging indictment in repudiation of their version of beauty. Consider the following passage:

Moreover, the LORD said, "Because the daughters of
Zion are haughty, and walk with heads held high, and
seductive eyes and go along with mincing steps, and jin-
gle the anklets on their feet, The Lord will afflict the
scalp of the daughters of Zion with scabs, And
the LORD will make their foreheads bare."

On that day, the Lord will take away the beauty
of *their* anklets, headbands, crescent ornaments, dan-
gling earrings, bracelets, veils, headdresses, ankle
chains, sashes, perfume boxes, amulets, finger
rings, nose rings, festive robes, outer garments, shawls,
purses, papyrus garments, undergarments, headbands,
and veils.

Now it will come about that instead of balsam oil there
will be a stench; Instead of a belt, a rope; Instead
of well-set hair, a plucked-out scalp; Instead of fine
clothes, a robe of sackcloth; *And* branding instead of
beauty.

Your men will fall by the sword and your mighty ones
in battle. And her gates will lament and mourn,
And she will sit deserted on the ground.

We must weigh beauty against the majesty of the Lord and the
teleology (divine purpose) He assigned to it. In this vein, the
creature is certain to give his Creator glory for the beautiful.

When we understand the origin of beauty, we must affirm and praise the work of the Creator behind it. For everything God creates is divine artistry raised for His glory and praise. The woman's beauty is not self-created, but divinely imposed through those properties designed for her and all things beautiful.

Properties of Beauty

As mentioned, the six fundamental properties of beauty, which are *Unity, Diversification, Hierarchy, Complexed Layers, Symmetry, and Form* are the exact constituents found in God's essence, because they originate from Him. Aesthetic properties are instinctual, they are naturally present in us. We do not confine them to the woman but are basic to anyone or anything that has beauty. Other researchers and scholars may use alternate terminology to describe these and may even expand beyond what is available here. However, the fundamentals of the properties of beauty are the same, and subsequently that which comprises the properties of a woman's beauty, which require a more intimate analysis.

Unity and Diversity

These are the two most significant essentials to the properties of beauty; in that they speak to foundational aspects or building blocks necessary for something beautiful. Every creative work of art begins with a clean slate, a blank page, a base, or a canvas of sorts. A blank page or canvas may appear idle and unmoving until you add various lines, shapes, and color.

Then the power of the canvas is notable in its ability to collect and tie lines, shapes, and colors into a cohesive artistic message. Unity and diversity are not only essential to the properties of beauty but are fundamental to human ontology (Being). That God created us in His image suggests that unity and diversity are fundamental to God's essence. The unity and diversity we naturally desire and seek is a divine paradox that originates and rests in Him. He is a "Tri-unity" Being, a Triune God and Creator; He is "three-in-oneness". This means that He is One Being, yet manifests in three persons. That God is One essence, and Three persons (Father, Son, and Holy Spirit) shows the aesthetic paradox of unity and diversity. Each person in the Trinity or Godhead exists eternally and is always fully God. Unity is one of God's incommunicable attributes.

Everything that God is, He is complete, without contradiction or compromise to any of His divine attributes. He possesses unity and diversity in a manner that no other living being can. Made in His image, it is only fitting that creation bare resemblance of this unity, but do not and cannot possess and express it fully or to the extent God does. For instance, God technically created humans with three beings. Consider I Thessalonians 5:23,

> Now may the God of peace Himself sanctify you entirely; and may your spirit, and your soul and body be preserved complete, without blame at the coming of our Lord Jesus Christ. (Emphasis is mine)[47]

Another example of diversity functioning as one entity (although not a complete explanation of the Trinity) is the automobile, which on average comprise 30,000 parts.[48] They operate in a unified way to function according to design. The distinction is that a part like that of an alternator is not the car, nor can it function as whole. It is always a part of the car, and cannot work independently, which makes it worthless without the other parts.

But the point in view here is that although seemingly paradoxical, unity and diversity work harmoniously as properties of beauty. That the woman is a multiphasic creature is indisputable. God created her with such distinction. Her diversity is clear, and notable through intelligence, talent, wisdom, and the blessings she imparts to others.

Hierarchy

We recognize hierarchy across multiple disciplines, i.e., social science, mathematics, theology, ethics, philosophy, and science. Hierarchy speaks to the proper order of things. For instance, priorities that are necessary for effective operation, a strategic arrangement of things to fulfill a duty or call, and to bring order to various elements of a composition. The etymology of the word itself derives from the Greek word ἱεραρχία (hierarkhia) meaning 'rule of a high priest', and from hierarkhes, which means 'president of sacred rites'. It includes the concept of arrangement, either as above, below, or same level as another. Hierarchy is the one concept and system that troubles the woman. Hierarchical abuse by her male-counterpart

pollutes her perception of the concept and direct experience of these causes her to interpret hierarchy as something negative. Because of this, some prefer that the system not exists or is up-ended to effect change. Notwithstanding, the misappropriation of instruments and systems injuriously does not make the instrument and system inherently evil or bad. The absence of integrity, respect and responsibility is at the heart of the issue. Although the chronicles of time showcase men using the system inappropriately, hierarchy did not ideate from man's fallen mind as an organized system to effect and preserve power and control. Rather, hierarchy, both as a concept and system, is in fact uncreated. Therefore, we cannot perceive it as a process propagated through human ingenuity. Hierarchy originates in God Himself; it began with Him. He is naturally a hierarchical Being.

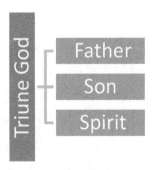

God then introduces hierarchy into creation, not man. The Creator's relationship to Himself is exemplary of this. The Father is above all, and the Son is subject to the Father, then the Spirit, yet all three are One, and the One, all three.

Another example confirming that hierarchy originates from God is apparent through the hierarchical system governing angels, whom we believe God created likely within the first second of that cataclysmic explosion he authors in the creation of the universe. Because angels were eyewitnesses to the rest of creation[49], including man, they had to exist prior to God's creation of earth and humanity, but did not exist prior to God's decision to create.[50]

As the first level of created order of beings, God designed angels within systems of rank and responsibilities. The terms thrones, dominions, rulers, or authorities noted in Ephesians 1:21; and Colossians 1:16 indicate rank and responsibility among angels. For instance, Jude 1:9 identifies an angel named Michael as the 'archangel', a term indicative of rank and authority. God's hierarchical system expands deeper into His creation. There are angels (who exists within their own rank and responsibility) then there are humans, who are lower than angels, yet exist in hierarchical system designed for them (i.e., man, woman, children) then the animal kingdom, who exist in a system that is lower than humans, yet all things are subject or under the Creator. Hierarchical systems show our relationship to the Creator, ultimately. This concept extends to various entities, such as church and government. Christ is Head of the church. Subject to Him are the offices of Elders, Ministers, Deacons, Teachers, and then, members.

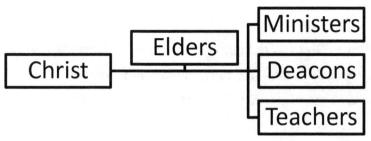

The entire world system and human experience exists in a hierarchical paradigm. Besides former examples are hierarchical systems in biology, morality and justice, and the human body itself, i.e., the head, which contains the brain, is higher anatomically and is more significant than the other parts of the body. Hierarchical systems (God's design) produce order and efficiency. It is no wonder that the woman has within her a hierarchical element and system through which her beauty radiates. When she functions according to the Creator's design and order for her, when a woman is a woman, the beauty of the Lord emanates through her being. God positioned her to provide the greatest impact she can offer to humanity. The woman, as well as everything He has created, reflects the hierarchical essence of her Creator.

Complexity (Layers)

If we took a microscopic view of everything that was ever created, we would find that everything has layers, meaning God composed them of multiple substances making that thing a functional whole. Further, careful analysis will also reveal that God created big and complexed things out of smaller things.

For instance, God created our infinitely vast and immeasurably complexed universe by fiat, meaning He spoke creation into existence. In the beginning, God 'created'...[51] The Hebrew word for created (Bara) means to bring something into existence, which suggests that it did not exist prior and therefore was "ex nihilo" which means "created out of nothing".[52] For decades physicist have rejected this notion, but admittedly note that the farther we travel back in space and time, we realize the universe derived from (what they dub "unknown energy") that produced an extremely tiny, infinitely dense point. The automobile begins with a frame and a building begins with a foundation. The human body has 78 organs[53], 12 parts or systems, of all of which derived from a handful of dust. It then is conceivable and sound to suggest that all things are the sum of its parts.

Keeping this concept in tow, let us go back to one of the major sections in chapter one, namely the creation of the woman. Remember, as Adam lingers under divine anesthesia, God takes bone, flesh and DNA and literally "built" the woman. As noted, the Hebrew word used for "fashioned" in Genesis 2: 22 means to build. I have already noted the distinctive way God created the woman. Who in their right mind living today can deny the fact that the woman is a mysteriously beautiful, complexed creation?

Her complexity is clear in her gracious spirit, usually soft personality, her approach to thought, reason, and decision-making,
the efficacy of her love and forgiving spirit. The basis for these
and the way they construct differ from her male-counterpart.
Albeit the world perpetually covets her love, forgiveness, support, and presence. Usually, the intricacy of a thing adds value
to it. We value art, buildings, and precious stones (in part) by
the intricacy that forms them. We value even a gourmet dish
higher because of its complex taste and structure. God created
the woman with complexed layers that give her functionality
and value. When these layers operate according to divine
standards, the beauty of the Creator shines through her.

Balance | Symmetry

It is said, "every work of beauty is balances; has proper proportions; and has visual equity."[54] In aesthetics, we also see
balance as the "unity between elements which, while they op-
pose or conflict with one another need or supplement each
other."[55] Any appreciation for balance as a critical property of
the woman's beauty requires understanding the concept of the
woman within the grand scheme of God's created order. Sometimes the average person (whether Christian) does not have a
real understanding of the significance of the woman to the created order. As I will point out in Chapter 8, the absence of
God's woman will tip humanity into a perilous chaos. Her mere
presence in the world help brings order, stability, tranquility,
and balance.

For this reason, God has equipped the woman with unique characteristics that move the created order closer to His divine purpose. Remember, the woman is not an afterthought. The concept of the woman did not rise out of Adam's perceptional emptiness. As mentioned earlier, God conceives the concept of the woman before the foundation of the world. This is significant to understanding how the Creator God operates. He did not make things up as He was creating the world. There were no "light bulb moments" in which He suddenly had a better idea; there were no errors prompting the need for correction, because He always sees the end at the beginning. His wisdom and knowledge are thorough and lacks nothing. The place, the role, and the mission of the woman came from her Creator and Him alone.

Guided by His own objectives, God gives the woman balancing characteristics, such as a love that is quantitively and qualitatively unique, patience, exceptional vision, talent, wisdom, motherhood (whether biological or otherwise) and much more. Through these she balances humanity. Her soft essence and spirit give man, family and community, balance; she is the other of him, purposefully. Remember, she is a strategically created specialty. For instance, there is another notable aspect of balance also presented in the woman, which is the fact that balance stresses difference, whether that difference is manifest by ethnicity, gender, social class, economic status, faith, or any conflicts rising between these.

Balance also contrasts character, which shows the importance of difference and contrast in any context. As an ontological property of beauty, balance helps establish harmony between things that contrast others. Men and women are not only different anatomically, but socially and in many other categories and contexts. When they live in union, or operate harmoniously, not only is the beauty of difference emphasized but the supplemental necessity of one for the other. Difference and contrast sometimes yearn for sameness. In this context, sameness and difference replace equality, which is often presented as "sameness". For harmony to exist between different elements (or Beings, in this case) there must be an identical quality or purpose (sameness) embedded in contrasting element or Being (difference). In short, there must be sameness in difference, just like there is diversity in unity.[56]

If balance is an innate property of beauty in the woman, it can only mean that it is teleological (has divine purpose) meaning God gave the woman balance for a specific end or reason, that when accomplished, her value is visible. Second, God's purpose for balance not only rests in the woman, but the man as well, for example. Remember, for harmony to exist between contrasting forces, "there must be an identical quality or purpose" in both. Here, divine purpose becomes the force drawing the man and woman into 'sameness'.

But harmony between the man and the woman is not the goal or end game, it is a means to an even greater end. Embedded into the concept of balance is functionality, which must progress to a valued end of divine reasons. When something functions to a valued end, that value has been pre-purposed by the source authoring it, in this case, God. God designs the woman to provide balance, to ensure the man and humanity-at-large functions properly. When she functions according to His design, she causes everything else in the human order to function properly, and all things instinctively glorify the Creator. When the woman is out-of-balance, it forges a domino effect on the home, community, church, and society, and dishonors God's objectives.

Form

This is not a reference to the woman's body, although it has form and is beautiful, it is not what is in view directly. Every corporeal and architectural structure has a form that naturally creates boundaries, parameters, or lines. The human body, automobiles, buildings, and airplanes are tangible examples of this. But here, form indicates that which embodies a unique essence, a compelling structure that is purpose driven, a hierarchical system of value, and the indelible intelligence, wisdom, and character emanating from it. God by nature has form. He is the origin of form, thus without Him, not only can we not understand form, but it cannot exist. Because of this, out of His infinite wisdom, He created humans with the capacity to

identify and appreciate this inherent property of beauty. A closer look at the components making up form highlights the woman's natural endowment of these traits.

- Unique essence. As mentioned in chapter one and two, the genetic code the Creator embeds into the woman orchestrates and produces an essence that is far distinctive than her male counterpart. The woman's unique nature is inexplicable, which others cannot duplicate, but only imitate. She is distinctively woman. She harnesses a delicacy unparalleled in the human experience, and that manifests consistently in heart, body, and spirit. One example of the woman's individuality is apparent through her oxytocin level and behavior in the amygdala, a vital component of the brain's limbic system controlling emotion and behavior. Oxytocin is a chemical in the brain found in men and women, and produces affection, love, and bonding.[57]

However, scientists have noted the distinctive way in which oxytocin behaves in this part of the woman's brain. It not only triggers the labor process for childbirth, but nurturing, bonding, and love in greater proportions than her counterpart. As mentioned in chapter one, the Creator gave this to the woman at the very beginning. Whether through traditional biological processes or unorthodox contexts, the woman's beauty animates when she nurtures bonds and expresses love to a degree in which only she can. The true love of a woman as a wife, mother, friend, and confidant is priceless, and sweetens the human experience.

- A compelling structure that is purpose driven. For something to be interesting, it must have a force within it; something unique about it that draws, that irresistibly beckons. As Creator and the supreme standard of beauty, God draws all things unto Himself, garnering praise, glory, and submission. Similarly, the essence of the woman undeniably compels or draws life and experience to herself. The woman's compelling structure is that which comprises her essence, her ontology. It is the quality of her love, and nurturing capacity; the unending pursuit of holiness and proper relationship with God; her concern for the other, which is manifested in her ongoing communal involvement. But any compelling structure that does not have purpose is meaningless, because it motions and motivates without cause, and to no end. When God draws His creation to Him, it is to effect relationship, to generate worship and glory, of which He is worthy.[58] Like her male-counterpart, the woman does not author her own compelling structure, but God Himself, who assigned purpose to this structure while constructing human existence. The woman's interesting features then, are teleological. Through the efficacy of love, nurturing, caring, and wisdom, she provides healing and direction for her community, honors God, and

invites others into awareness and covenant relationship with Him, all of which is His will for the woman. But as mentioned in previous chapters, by God's permission, all humans are sovereign beings, in that God created us with will, and the capacity to decide about behavior independently. Again, God does not force us into relationship with Him, He invites us into a covenant relationship. It then is up to every human to decide on their own, whether to accept His invite[59] or decline. One has a reward, the other, consequence, but both are a matter of choice and will.

- <u>A hierarchical system of value.</u> One of the prominent composites of hierarchy is categorization, namely of ability, responsibility, and status (status as it pertains to one's "operational position" to another). Although there is a constant push for equality, sameness, and equilibrium in every context and dimension of life, the development of form as an integral property of beauty rises out of diversity. Here, human reasoning usually obscures the true meaning of value systems. In our finite minds, placing seemingly more value on one thing involuntarily minimizes or invalidates the value of the other, which is not accurate necessarily. Human tendency to perceive and process everything within the parameters of personal desire and experience, forfeits the richness of the created order. All things exist in order or in relation to the Creator. There is a natural hierarchical system in creation. Everything within the created order operates within hierarchical systems, which give life to form. The Creator determines the creature's rank and responsibility, which God predicates on their relation to Him, the abilities He gives them and the purpose for them. For instance, angels created as ministering spirits to aid the work of God[60], rank higher (at least in ability and holiness) than humans, and humans in relation to God are higher than the animal kingdom. In addition, in their relationship to God, the man and the woman rank according to their ontology and the teleological orders assigned to each one. But all things are subject to God as Creator.

As each created being functions within their divine purpose, various forms emerge, and their value, which is determined by the Creator, is notable. The value system assigned to the woman by God during her creation contributes to the quality of form found in her properties of beauty. The divine purpose upon which the hierarchical system of value rests, highlights and distinguishes form.

- Intelligence, wisdom, and character. That humans have a capacity for intelligence and are intelligent beings is testament to a Creator and His communicable attributes. This refers to those attributes God electively shares with His creation. Communicable attributes such as intelligence, love, holiness and will, to name a few, are attributes that originate from Him and shared with creation to a limited extent.[61]

There is no other being greater in intellect, wisdom, or any other communicable attribute. Although He shares these with us, no one is equal to or greater than He is in any area. Besides these are those attributes that are incommunicable, meaning these attributes rest with God only because He does not share them with anyone or anything. For instance, His aseity or self-existence, uncreated status, eternity, extensive knowledge of all things, the capacity to exist everywhere, simultaneously and Omnipotence[62] are important examples of incommunicable attributes.

Wisdom and intelligence produce a character that give body and identity to form. One hallmark of a woman's beauty and grace develops out of the wisdom she possesses. When the woman shares grace and wisdom, they are influential moments in which the beauty of the Lord shines through. The wisdom of a mother or a wife (like that of Abigail in chapter two) are valuable contributions to the human experience. The greater the individual's wisdom and intelligence, the more distinctive and higher the form. For instance, man has more intelligence than animals. Conversely, animals are lower forms of creation. Wisdom and intelligence produced meaningfully gives form identity. The woman's intelligence, wisdom and character produce a distinctive form and ensures her value in the created order.

The valuable properties that coalesce to produce the woman's beauty reflect the Holy One, whose beauty surpasses human knowledge and wisdom. This then invalidates ethnicity, race, body size or type, hair, education, social and economic status as valuable factors of beauty. In every instance in which the woman taps into these precious properties that are both indispensable and innate, she places God on display. The properties of a woman's beauty are the tale sign and mark of a beautiful Lord and Creator. Through the beauty of the woman, God makes His presence known and His mission certain. Unity and Diversity, Hierarchy, Complexity, Balance and Form, originate from God's essence.

The next time a beautiful woman comes into view, it is not a "catcall" that is in order, but a show of reverence to the woman, and a salute of praise, honor, and glory to the Highest, and an expression of gratitude for His providence, grace, and love, which are clearly manifest in such divine artistry in the woman. The most beautiful woman is the one who displays her alignment with her inner divinity.

The providence of God dwells in women
all over the world

The Divinity of the Woman

A Measure of God with Us

In Christian theological contexts, divinity points to the state of quality of being divine or something perceived to be godly; or most often, God's nature or character. We also perceived it as a thing that is related, devoted to or that proceeds from deity.[1] One impression hopefully already captured in this writing is the fact that the woman's unique ontology derives from a Divine Creator. If we study God's actions critically, the notion that He orchestrates everything from beginning to end; from top to bottom is clearly visible. It gives reason to why all that He desires and commands always happens. Although He allows humans to take part in His divine plan, we are subject to His Sovereign Will. No human, angelic being, or any other power can ultimately thwart the plans of God. Everything that is conceived in His mind, and then falls from His lips, is unstoppable. Note:

So will My word be which goes forth from My mouth; It will not return to Me empty, without accomplishing what I desire, and without succeeding in the matter for which I sent it. -Isaiah 55: 11 (NASB)

This remains true even in the face of the sovereignty He has given us over our own will and behavior. Even though we are free to make our own decisions about behavior, and about when and how to respond to God's call, none of our decisions, nor their outcomes, will upend what He has purposed in His heart. God will ultimately have His way, period.

While keeping this thought in tow, as I have showed at several points throughout this writing, the motivation and blueprint for the creation sequence, God conceives in His mind prior to Genesis 1:1 ("In the beginning..."). Again, the word beginning as used here does not mean the beginning of God (because He is uncreated, He has no beginning) rather, it signals a critical point before the beginning of time and space. During this period, discussion develops within the Triune God to create a people to whom God the Father can offer as a love gift[2] to God the Son[3], a people presented ultimately and essentially to and for Himself.[4]

When he started and orchestrated the process to establish the universe, and tailored His work subsequently, the woman, (her ontology, capacity, and aim) gleamed in His mind like fresh ink from an architect's pin and precision. The earth, created within the context of the universe, is prepared first, as a suitable habitat for the people God wanted for Himself, a people made for His pleasure and glory.[5] When the earth was ready, God signaled the moment for the insoluble and historic creation of man. In the wake of His blueprint for humanity, and His divine purpose for them, God builds the woman in a way that includes Him as a part of her.

Remember, one property of the woman's beauty is balance, in which the concept of functionality is visible. In addition, the notion that this functionality contributes to "a valued end", a teleological end is equally exceptional here. She functions in a way to assist God's agenda, which He consistently leads her into. Scripture clarifies God will not leave any aspect of His overarching goal for humanity totally in the hands of humans themselves. Humans are too flawed and inept to accomplish God's plan for them independently. The Lord will always guide His divine agenda, the process, and people involved to a desired outcome.

To certify the human experience does not invalidate His objectives, God deposits a part of Himself into humanity, in which certain aspects are unique to the woman. After the Creator embeds these into her ontology, the woman becomes a measure of God with us. The woman's divinity has raised questions in the minds of some theologians, scholars, scientists, and other investigators regarding whether she uniquely possesses a more significant measure of God than her male-counterpart. Through the years, the woman's devotion to her Creator is seemingly more apparent than the male. For decades researchers have inquired, are women more religious than men?[6] One blaring premise for the question is apparent by the percentage of women in worship services, and their involvement in church activities. Women holding prominent positions in secular leadership are more often less corrupt than her male-counterpart holding the same positions. They are more subject to express godlike kindness more often and are more inclined to assist the needed, volunteer and take part in the wellbeing of others.

Research has long since validated women are more loving and have greater nurturing tendencies and capacity than men, qualities that originate from God. In its 2014 report (U.S. Religious Landscape Study[7]) the Pew Research Center investigates the question. Among Pew Research's findings was the notion that women are more religious than men, at least with Christians in the U.S.

The report specifically notes that 72% of women believe religion and faith are significant, while 62% of men made the same claim. 80% of Christian women claim certainty about God's existence; compared to 70% of Christian men. The report found that 74% of women pray daily, compared to 60% of men.

In every category in this study, there is a gender gap in which women lead men. Notwithstanding, interestingly, there is one group (Mormons) in which there is no significant gap between men (84%) and women (86%) in these categories.

Extensive research over the years has yet to produce definitive outcomes regarding reasons for the gender difference in religion. According to Pew Research, there is some sign that this gap has narrowed to within 6 points.[8] However, women still lead in the related categories. The data that lends itself to potential reasons or theories for this phenomenon falls into three expanded categories: nature, nurture, or mosaic (a combination of these).

Nature

This theory suggests physiological causes such as those produced by hormones, genes or "biological predispositions"[9], may provide some explanation for gender differences in religion. For instance, one expert points to elevated risk taking commonly produced by male testosterone, as a viable explanation why men are usually less religious than women.[10] The idea then, is that women are more religious because of naturally lower testosterone levels. The observation that men appear more likely to risk not being punished for their sins in the afterlife is the premise for such spiritual risks.[11] Although undetermined, some scientists believe "biological predispositions" may explain varied religiosity between genders.[12]

Nurture

This theory focuses on the impact of socialization into conventional gender roles, the extent to which women engage the workforce, and "national economic structures".[13] Some social scientists believe social facts that point to childbirth and dying predicate gender difference in religiosity, which in effect causes women particularly to stay closer to God than their male-counterpart. In addition, some of these same scientists believe pressure on the woman to be religious as a mechanism to control female sexuality explains the difference in religiosity. Although they note this aspect as one explanation for the difference between men's and women's religiosity, the fact God did not design faith and religion to be used in this manner is noteworthy. Any man or group that uses the Word of God in ways He has not ordained will suffer major consequences.

The caveat for the woman is to ensure she does not reject the words of her Creator in response to the injudicious behavior of men, for which too there is consequence. In addition, according to Pew Research Center, Marta Trzebiatowska and Steve Bruce of the University of Aberdeen, note that given the male's "pre-eminent role" in society, the impact from contemporary secularization[14] manifest in men first.[15] In its wake is an altered view of God, religion, faith, and church, which for them are no longer seen as plausible. When people live by rules and values that are formed by their communities and outside normative Christian contexts, and experience satisfactory levels of success, church and or God becomes obsolete, at least in its traditional form.

Given this, the number of men professing faith in God and attending church regularly were lower than women who were less employed or educated. As noted, additional research reveals the gap between men and women's religiosity has significantly narrowed. Interestingly, during the same period in which this gap narrows, women were more educated and employed. The inference then, is that as soon as women became just as educated, employed, and guided by the same secularized norms and values, their interest in religiosity declined just like their male-counterpart. There are some studies in which the findings suggest that the lower the number of working women, the greater their religious commitment.[16] Another related study finds educated women with high paying, full-time jobs less religious, largely because of minimal "social validation and acknowledgement" from their faith communities.[17]

The Mosaic

In the absence of definitive data connecting the physical, biological differences between men and women as a valid explanation for the religiosity gap; and the persistence of such gaps in the face of social factors, scientists surmise it is too complex to know definitively, and suggests that it might be a combination of both nature–nurture concepts. Notwithstanding their data, I lean toward the concept of a greater manifestation of God in the woman as suggested by her DNA. Greater not in superior context, but an increased aspect of ontology to a functional end. For instance, the woman has a greater capacity to love and nurture, certainly more than her male-counterpart.

In chapters one and two, I highlight the unique contributions God gave the woman to a functional end. The physical and biological tenets scientists are flirting with may in fact hold information that will point to the natural structure of the woman, and in effect provide credence to her divinity.

A Threefold Manifestation

One point critical to understanding this chapter is in the concept regarding God's sovereignty or independence. As mentioned, the Lord directs every aspect of His plans, especially those that have to do with us humans. For instance, when He made Adam from dust, He had no intentions of making just one human being. The plan was to raise a people for the purposes He outlined before the beginning of time. Grabbing dust from the ground billions of times over to create the people His heart desired was not on His agenda.

Instead, He equips the male and female with capacity for reproduction, within which He gives the woman greater responsibility and resources. God develops His plan through the life and experience of humanity. We then (whether or not we want to be) are 'helpers', aids to a divine agenda.

The divinity of the woman is not only emblematic of a Divine Creator but also one medium through which His presence exists in humanity. While He is primarily present with His people through the Holy Spirit, He is also uniquely present in the world through the woman. As the Sovereign Creator of the universe, He could have chosen any medium through which to enter the world, but preferably Jesus Christ entered the world through a woman.[18] This infers that while He was creating the first woman in the Garden of Eden, He was well aware of His plan for her to become the conduit through which human life would develop and enter the world; and she would be the memorable channel through which He Himself enters the world to save humanity.

God subsequently arranges the woman's anatomy and ontology for such a glorious advent, which predisposes her to a preordained function and outcome. Her divinity then has more to do with how God manifests through her. That she is a chosen vessel of the Lord always warrants reverence, if not for her directly, then certainly for His presence in her, and the unique role and reason for her existence. If the world sees the woman through this prism, it will correctly assess her ontological value, and society will revolutionize how it approaches and interacts with the woman. Given her ontological value and the unique essentials embedded by the Creator, her divinity is a measure of God living among people.

The divinity of the woman manifests in three ways:

1) As the '**helper**'. If there is any word that usually offends the 21st century woman and causes her to throw her hands on her hips in disgust and protest, 'helper' is likely near the top of the list! Why then include the word in this writing, you ask? Because the word needs to be understood in its proper meaning and context. The degrading behavior of men in antiquity and contemporary times mar and obscure the beauty and significance of the word. It is the fallout of effecting Holy Scripture as an instrument of power and control to an egotistical end. But here, the wisdom of the woman must power through, by differentiating the corrupt behavior of men, from the mission of her Creator. The concept of a 'helper' derives from God, not man. Note.

   Then the Lord God said, "It is not good for the man to be alone; <u>I will make him a helper suitable</u> for him." Genesis 2:18 (NASB)

   The creation of man is only one half of what is necessary for God's agenda. He needed 'help' to complete the mission assigned to him by God. Adam's form correlates with his divine assignment, just as the woman's form correlate with hers. This also tells us that God knew in advance that the form in which he made the first human as one aspect necessary for His mission, and that a second creature with unique qualities would in fact complete the picture. God is a God of relation, He is a relational Being (Father, Son, and Holy Spirit).

Although limited, the relationship between man, woman, and their Creator produces a similar concept. But the most beautiful aspect of the word (helper) is nestled in the word's meaning in Hebrew, and its application and affiliation to the Divine Creator. For instance, in Psalm 115:9-11 and Psalm 121:1-2, this same word 'help' applied to women describes God.

O Israel, trust in the Lord; He is their *help* and their shield. O house of Aaron, trust in the Lord; He is their *help* and their shield. You who fear the Lord, trust in the Lord; He is their help and their shield. Ps. 115:9-11

I will lift up my eyes to the mountains; From where shall my help come? My help comes from the Lord, Who made heaven and earth. Psalm 121:1-2

There are no derogatory words ever assigned to or affiliated with God... something not even Satan would do! What we see here is a holy Creator electing to live and orchestrate His plan through the body, mind, and spirit of the woman. She is, in fact, a measure of God with us. The concept of a helper, include the idea of support, and for something to function as support requires capacity, strength, wisdom, and knowledge equal to, if not greater than, the thing supported. The idea of a helper is not a negative notion on its face. Designation as a 'helper' is in effect to be what God is to humanity.

2) The **uniqueness of the woman's love** is the second medium in which God is present and manifest through her divinity. When a woman loves, it is one of the best experiences within the human realm, whether it is maternal, benevolent, or romantic. Her love nurtures, soothes, heals, pardons, and affirms. The efficacy of her love pours out from her unique ontology. As mentioned, we now know that oxytocin is the powerful source behind the woman's maternal behavior.[19] These maternal instincts are present in women who are mothers biologically and in those who have adopted or parent blended families. In fact, scientific data suggests that women who give birth and women who are mothers via adoption or some other unorthodox context, are equally "biological mothers" because the hormones that prime women to respond to stimuli requiring maternal qualities are present and active in both types of. mothers.[20]

Why does a woman with biological children and one with children through nontraditional mediums have the same maternal instincts? Because the Creator embedded into the woman's DNA hormones like oxytocin. They are innate to the woman. Her tendency the love in this way, is a by-product of a Creator who loves. Love began with God, for He is love. Again, we say God is love[21], not that it is a feature of His Being, rather, it is His essence.

Through the ontology of the woman, God reaches into humanity to nurture, protect, and provide for humanity. Love has characteristics suited for the human experience, i.e., patience, kindness, humility, unselfishness, perseverance, strength, forgiveness, hope and faith.[22]

When the woman exhibits these, she becomes like her Creator, her God in that moment. He extends Himself to the world through the woman.

3) The **woman's providential nature** is the third medium in which God is manifest in her and present in the world, as such. The woman's foresight, wisdom, her discretion, and economy aimed at her own and the good of the other, is reminiscent of a God who is also Father, providing, caring, and protecting those who are His. The woman carries within her so many characteristics of Divinity, all of which are provided as means to a divine end. Made to exist and primarily function according to divine order, she has within her the greatest possession, characteristics of Holy God who seeks to love and care for His own. The divinity of the woman is a measure of God with us, and by this, she is a vital treasure to humanity.

Humanity is better served when it sees God's presence and works through the woman.

The Woman is strategically created and ordained to affect the human experience positively.

Inverted Appraisal

Rehabilitating the Collective's Value Matrix of the Woman

*T*he indelible notion that the woman is a "created specialty" and an indispensable contribution to humanity should serve as a consult guiding all human perception and exchange with her unique ontology. But rummaging through the coffers of antiquity, characteristics of a moral miscarriage are too pungent to ignore. Although (as the adage has it) "time heals all things" it does not remove scars left from traumatic episodes within the human agenda.

Even during intermission precipitated by the woman's inevitable and irrefutable rise to power, and truncated concessions by her male- counterpart, the devaluation of many women creeps constantly. The evolution of society, in which the zenith of academics, technology, medicine, and wealth are hallmarks, certifies the undeniable progress of people and their cause.

But rusty scalpels that still trash fields of change and recovery constantly threatened the upward movement of people and groups; scalpels that were used historically to carve away composites of a woman's value.

The enduring plight of the woman as a woman is unavoidably engrained in our communities and psyches today. Modern headlines, reading like the annals of ancient periods, are vivid reminders of this. But the million-dollar question is why does this cinema feature the same reel, century after century? Believe it or not, there are three logical explanations for this attitudinal approach and behavior, 1) demoniacal forces, 2) divine adjudication, and 3) an inverted appraisal, the first of which surfaces in the early chapters of this writing. But because two of the reasons develop out of the first, it is helpful to review all of them here.

Reason One (Demonic Forces)

The first reason for the inequitable life of the woman develops out the accession and actual existence of demonic forces, a fact too often minimized and ignored. You are likely pondering how this has anything to do with the plight of the woman, a connection I will make shortly. The world must concede that there is an unseen realm in play around us and has a serious impact and implication for life and death. Every sane person knows that every human will one day die. Death that is truly actual results from permanent separation of the body and soul or spirit.[1] While we leave the body behind, the soul enters a new world, the Unseen realm. The term "Unseen" is not something contemporary theologians invented. Rather, it derives from the prefix and noun form of the Greek word Hades, and in this form refers to the entire "Unseen" realm in which every disembodied being exists.

For instance, in Revelation 1:18, Jesus Christ notes "... I have the keys of death and of Hades." Here, Hades refers to the entire "Unseen" world. What Christ is saying is that He controls the Unseen world, which certifies its existence. On a prior occasion, He noted the "gates of Hell" (which in Greek means the "council of the Unseen") will not overpower the church.[2, 3] In this Unseen realm, God, holy angels, and the righteous dead (meaning those who died while in covenant relationship with the Lord[4]) are in the section called heaven; fallen angels (meaning those who disobeyed God, such as those mentioned in II Peter 2:4 and Jude 1:6) are in a temporary prison of sorts, known as 'Tartarus' in Greek. The wicked dead (meaning, those who *consistently* disobeyed God and rejected Jesus Christ, in effect) are in a different section of Hell.

But there is one aspect of the Unseen realm that is not only troubling for the woman, but humanity collectively, the section including the atmosphere of the earth and the bottomless pit. This is where Satan and his demons live.[5, 6] This concept is not some sort of science fiction phenomenon, employed to exploit the fears and dreams of the masses. Satan and his demons are real. One cannot believe in God and dismiss the concept of an Unseen realm and other inhabitants.

When Satan and his demons' attempted coup failed in heaven, the genesis of the battle between evil and good, darkness and light, made its mark in time and space. Satan, sore over his failure and God's swift punishment, which threw him and other angels who succumbed to his foolish desire and antics, into the bottomless pit; is now bent on destroying the work of God. He knows well that it is impossible to defeat and destroy the Creator, and that God is going to destroy him at the appointed time.[7] He constantly attempts to disrupt God's plan by taking down as many of His people and creation as possible.

By almost any means necessary, the evil one works feverishly to upend the work of God, including blinding people from the truth, and holding them in bondage to desires that obstructs relationship with God.[8] In one attempt to sabotage God's plan, Satan's demons tried to contaminate the lineage leading to the birth of Christ.[9] As Wayne Grudem notes, Satan and his crew will use "temptation, doubt, guilt, fear, confusion, sickness, envy, pride, and slander"[10], to name a few, to thwart God's agenda.

Remember, Satan, along with the other angels, watched God create the world and the first humans. He understood the woman to be a significant aspect of God's created order and plan. This is clear by his initial approach and offensive. The Genesis account notes that Satan does not begin his attack with Adam, the man, but Eve, the woman. This move signals a subliminal message in which an irrefutable concession of the woman's value to the Creator's theocratic commission is manifest. As a critical component, God's structure and hierarchical system protect the woman throughout her earthly experience. This protection has nothing to do with weakness or competency, but signals value, significance, and specialism. It is not uncommon to guard, protect, and finesse something that is valuable, exceptional, or important.

Enter any museum in the world, you will find artifacts, precious stones and jewelry protected and handled delicately because of its value and special character. The Secret Service heavily guards the president and vice-president whenever they travel around the country and the world, not because of weakness, but their valued positions and importance to government and country.

This is the case with the woman. God made provisions for her protection by introducing a system into the world. It was not because of weakness, but the delicate nature and significance of her ontology to His plan for humanity.

As mentioned in previous chapters, the biblical text does not explain why Eve was alone when Satan approached; we do not know where Adam was during this critical moment. But what is clear, Satan exploited the opportunity, and given the significance of the woman to God's plan, he likely sought it out. Between Adam's absence, Eve's desire to Be, Become, and Belong, the protection put in place for the woman was inaccessible during this life altering encounter. Therefore, God cursed the "human experience". For years, many have taught and believed that, because of their transgressions, Adam and Eve receive the curse. But if you look at the text closely (Genesis 3:1-15) you see it is not the man that is cursed, but the ground from which he will now toil. After God had placed him in paradise and provided everything he needed, the consequence of his sin evicts him, and he now faces the drudgery of work, a decaying world, difficulty, sickness, and death eventually. In addition, God did not curse

Eve, but her "human experience" beginning with the birthing process, in which the pain experienced is "multiplied", a truth applicable unto this day. The next consequence God imposes sets up the second reason for the woman's inequitable human experience—divine adjudication.

Reason Two (Divine Adjudication)

Perhaps everything God has declared in consequence of Adam and Eve's decisions and actions He includes in this divine adjudication. But the consequence that exasperates not only the woman's earthly challenge, but the man's, is in what God says immediately following declaring intense pain during childbirth[11], i.e.,

> Yet your desire will be for your husband, and he will rule over you. -Genesis 3:16 (NASB)

In this second look at this text, let us refocus on three critical terms, "desire", "husband", and "rule". As mentioned earlier, part of God's adjudication includes difficulty in the relationship between the man and the woman that did not exist before the fall. By introducing sin into the world by them, the beautiful harmony designed for marriage and relationship between the sexes defaces and becomes difficult to achieve independent of critical essentials God has ordained for successful relationship.[12] In the wake of all of this, life became much harder to experience peacefully, joyfully, and live harmonically as originally intended.

The three critical words identified in the text above bring this reality into view. As mentioned, the word desire originates from Hebrew term (T^{e}shuqah) and means "stretching out after, a yearning, a longing"[13] in reality, to want something intensely. Although this type of desire can include a sexual context, this is not what is in view here, primarily. Because the next word, husband not only refers to a mate, but manliness. Besides, sexual desire already existed between them prior to the fall. God would not have used this as an outcome of disobedience. The desire must be a longing for something other than sex. Remember, chapter one notes that the Hebrew word for the woman is Ishasha, which is a derivative of the man, i.e., wo-man. The Hebrew word for man is "Ish" which means man.[14] This is how we know that God's view of a husband is always a man, a male.

We do well if we do not miss the connection between the words in this text. God shows that one consequence for the woman's sin is "desire" (to stretch out after long for) her husband, ("Ish") which means not only a mate, but manliness. Given that the desire as used in this text does not implicate sexual context, the latter meaning of the Hebrew "Ish" must be in view. The woman now desires the manliness commonly associated with her male-counterpart, i.e., dominion, leadership, strength, etc. Not that she (as a woman) is void of these, but that they become a coveted outcome, against and above the man, the husband. Before the fall, the woman and the man were co-rulers in God's universe. But divine adjudication altered the original arrangement and order, which sets up the final word- "rule".

Do take note that the word "rule" is for the husband, the man. It originates from the word Mashal in Hebrew; and means to reign, to govern, to have dominion, to manage. There is nothing in the word suggesting to lord over in an insensitive, demeaning, and harmful way. Rather, the fundamentals of governing or managing something are in view. But here is the problem, although God's adjudication changes the woman's original role to that of a "vice" of sorts, she (as a woman) now has a mindset in which she covets and will pursue dominion, which sets up a perpetual clash with the man. Because he will by nature seek to maintain dominance in all things, there is predilection toward over-reach, which can lead to devaluation and injury.

Man's natural tendency to dominate sets up conditions that contribute to the woman's inequitable human experience. The battle between the male and female will last until the end of time. The only way to resuscitate the harmonious relationship God intended for humanity is to embrace those principles he ordained for good relationship, whether in marriage or community with each other.

Reason Three (Inverted Appraisal)

The third reason for the woman's inequitable human experience sets up the context for the chapter title, Inverted Appraisal. The most significant aspect of an appraisal is its approximation or estimation of value. Realtors commonly use the word regarding professional services to determine the value of land or property. In short, it is value.

There are two questions I believe worthy of entertaining while navigating this section, i.e., what are the constituents of value? Can a person value something or someone without benefiting directly? Most people's estimation of value depends solely on how something or someone benefits them or improves their own outcome or net worth in some capacity. Maybe there is not anything wrong with that to an extent. But should that be the measure or standard to everything we assign value? Is a thing only valuable if we possess it, or profit from it? Is not the Pink Star Diamond, auctioned at Sotheby's for $71.2 million[15] still worth its dollar value whether you own it? Is it possible to assign value to something or someone that creates sacrifice for us to have or experience?

There are two factors contributing to the constituents or ingredients used to form value. One has to do with her male-counterpart's failure to see her "right-side up"; the other factor is her appraisal of self through a rearview ideology. There is significant language and space in this writing highlighting the true origin of a woman's value. In chapter two, we learn that the Creator (and Him alone) set the ontological value of the woman during her creation event. This subsequently implies that it is impossible to improve or diminish value assigned to her by God Himself. This can only mean that one part of what has happened to the woman historically and what we are witnessing in modern day is an inversion of those inalienable ingredients that make up her value.

When something is "inverted" it becomes rearranged from its original structure or design. What was right-side up is now upside down, what was down is now up, the inside is out, and the order of some things is reversed detrimentally.

The man's failure to see the woman as a "created specialty", a Being strategically built and ordained to affect the human experience positively, stains God's agenda. In the wake of such failure, authentic value of the woman becomes misplaced, and hides her injuries beneath the man's desires and acquisitions. Because the matrix of his appraisal of her is too often saturated with selfishness and insensitivity, he does not hold the divinity of the woman in view. Failing to see the woman through the lens of her Creator obscures value already assigned to her.

The woman has a novel experience but similar outcome, that is an inverted appraisal. It develops out of a matrix which is built around what I call "rearview ideology". This suggests that because of her human experience (her male-counterpart, specifically) the woman's view of value processes through concepts of equality, access, acquisition, and freedom. Denial of these is processed as devaluation. While these are available to the woman, and certainly her God-given right to demand and pursue, they do nothing to her true value. Because the ontological value of the woman comes from her Creator, which no man can improve or diminish. The things the woman seeks and desires most often will unquestionably improve her human experience, but her value remains unaffected. Whether she experiences all that she desires, and gains those things most significant to her, the ontological value given to her will not change. She is forever a "created specialty" with beauty, power, and divinity.

However, her persistent pursuit and the man's constant effort to dominate, perpetuate conflict, clash, and their fallout, making the human experience tough and inequitable; and demands God's presence and power to forage harmony between the man, the woman, and their Creator. Interestingly, there is an egotistical approach to appraisal by male and female alike. As mentioned, personal desire, goals, and heighten motivation by one's culture usually shape people's view of what is valuable. Therefore, in any context in which either the environment or its constituents are no longer seen or experienced as a viable means to a person's endgame, there is a loss of significance or a loss of value.

An appraisal system producing value that benefits more than just the individual seeking it, but the larger community, must have the following components:

- A base from which love and dignity of others are clear. Jesus noted, "love your neighbor, as yourself." Matthew 22:36-40. The word "neighbor" used here refers to not only the person immediately next door, but your countryman, the stranger, the other; people within your proximate sphere.[16]

- It must have an element of reciprocity, in which equality and fairness end is for the other, i.e., "Treat

people in the same way in which you want to be treated." Matthew 7:12.

- Should not be contradictory, i.e., expressing love toward one group of people, but hating others.

- It must be conciliatory, providing room for pardon and reconciliation. Eph. 4: 31-32.

- There must be consistency that benefits the greater good. Keeping the needs of others and community will ensure one's appraisal is adequate for everyone.

While this is not exhaustive, it helps produce the love, harmony, and tranquility between people as God intended. The only way to not see and treat the woman with the ontological value assign to her by God, is to invert measures design to appraise human worth. But if we these mediums properly, her true value is unavoidably apparent.

If the woman was insignificant to God's created order, she would not exist...

The Missing Madam

A Menace to Society

There are contexts or situations in which people do not recognize or appreciate the value of something until it is no longer accessible. Sometimes the simplest things or people with the mildest impact can create a gaping hole in life and community, in the wake of their absence. In other instances where we know the value of something or someone, its constant accessibility can cause some benefactors to take its worth for granted. Too often people value the experience or benefit from something but show little regard toward the source. When a person devalues another human, they essentially attempt to cheapen that individual's worth, or sadder, attempt to cancel any value previously assigned to that person.

Some may not understand that value and meaning connect intrinsically. Value produces meaning because within it is the undeniable reality of significance or consequence. Devaluation of another human or group then, suggests they are meaningless, their lives or being do not matter. In an era in which people erroneously superimpose ethnicity, race, and gender into the

calculus used for constructing meaning, few (if any) weigh the absence of such benefit in their environment. Blinded by selfishness, hate, and the desire to cause harm, there are groups who prefer others not exist. Staking a position without a comprehensive view of the consequence is foolish. For instance, elite groups tripping over themselves to ensure the plight of minorities is unproductive and uncomfortable as possible, really prefer that this population would vanish, or not inhabit their environment, at least. But the average person peddling this concept is likely oblivious to the fact that minority markets (Blacks, Hispanics, and Asians) hold 3.9 trillion in buying power annually.[1] Sudden vacuum of this magnitude will create a seismic shift many do not want and for which they are completely unprepared, including the cascading effects on the production of goods and services that elite groups rely so heavily upon. Total absence of minority groups will give birth to depths of misery unknown in modern times.

While one may think the total absence of minority groups is a stunning prospect, it pales compared to any hypothesis featuring the absence of the woman, or the missing madam[2]. By now (at least in this writing) the woman's ontological value and presence in society is clear. But incredibly, even in the face of this undeniable truth, are those who exhibit hate toward the woman and prefer too, that she did not exist or did not use their environment as much as she does. This is unquestionably another concept built out of foolish timber! If the woman no longer existed, whether by the hands and desire of her male-counterpart, or self-destruction, her mere absence threatens society as we know it. For this reason, I have entitled this chapter, The Missing

Madam, a Menace to Society. Given the woman's essential existence, it is difficult to pacify any wonder or notion of her nonexistence. However, to stress the absurdity of the idea, highlight potential consequences, and increase awareness of the woman's value to society, I will briefly note three critical areas in which her absence leverages the greatest impact, and threatens society's wellbeing subsequently. This ensemble includes economic, family, and spiritual contexts. It is unrealistic for anyone to assume or believe that the woman's absence will not produce dire consequences. If she were not significant to God's created order, she would not exist. He would not have created her. But the fact she exists speaks volumes about her importance and God's perception of the same.

Before detailing a few of the effects of the woman's absence in society, that definition of the word "absence" can include "deficiency" is noteworthy. Deficiency suggests vacant quality, inadequate essentials for health, whether financial, social, physical, or spiritual. Although attention to the "missing madam" is a direct fallout from a male-malfunction, the un-nerving reality that the absence of the woman also forages through self-destruction is noteworthy. During those unfortunate instances when the woman elects to live in contradiction to the principles of life ordained by her Creator, in which she abandons maternal responsibilities for the vertical chase for success; and sees eligibility and process as her own righteousness, and the acquisition of it, heaven; she mellows into a passion for being and belonging, at the expense of becoming. When engulfing desire and immorality, dazzling eyelashes and events tailored to taste emerge as the coveted goal of each passing week;

when her personal rise to power independently fuels her interest in the community, which obscures the need for genuine care of others; when she sees the church as a place for opportunity rather than a space for personal sacrifice; this "madam" has drifted down a road that leads to self-destruction, creating a vacuum that affects her immediate environment and society. But again, irrespective of the medium through which the woman's absence emerges, it affects society critically.

Family

It is of no surprise to anyone that the chief impact of the woman's absence is apparent in the family. Gifted with a special ontology, the woman is the backbone to the family unit. This is no more apparent than in her unique ability to nurture and support family. The UN Women's "flagship report" Families in a Changing World: Progress of the World's Women 2019-2020, provides a global snapshot of the status of women. It chronicles the impact of the woman's inequitable human experience on the family.[3] Among a plethora of global facts highlighting the issue, the increasing number of women delaying marriage to later in life, coupled with declining number of women entering marriage all together is most notable, because this affects the family unit directly. As a secularized exposition, the report does not speak to the woman's fidelity to faith in this context or whether faith exists among those targeted in the report.

Notwithstanding, God ordained the woman as an essential element for the framework and foundation of family. Through Adam, God gave the first woman the name Eve to signify motherhood and life through the woman,[4] to which God specifically created her. It suffices to say that birthing and nurturing are not the only dimensions of the woman. However, that as the agent through which human life develops, the physical absence of the woman will translate to the end of life, but her ontological absence has even greater impact. Even within the family structure, the woman is significant. In I Timothy 5:14 (a text that give many women grief because of its historical usage) the Greek word for guide (as in "guide the house") has concepts of authority, leadership or administration embedded into its definition, which suggests she plays a vital role in building and directing the home. Sociologists have long sensed measure the impact of the absence of the woman's involvement in the home.

Domestic labor seems an antiquated concept in this modern day. But the fact children are first conditioned and equip for society in the family or within the home makes the domestic front a critical entity for healthy societies. It is here (traditionally) that attitudinal frameworks develop; where people learn to overcome their fears; where we realize significance of guidance, love, and care for others; and likely the first place where the efficacy of morality emerges. Through the annals of time, the woman has always overwhelmingly shaped the lives of others. She counsels her children when to be afraid, and when to stand courageously, and how to be compassionate. For instance, I remember vividly one period during adolescence when I had an encounter with a bully in the neighborhood. Somehow my mother was aware of my brushes with the kid on the block. It is still a mystery how mothers come to know what kids work so hard to hide. Previous encounters with this kid ended up with me running in the house (likely out of fear) to avoid further escalation. But one afternoon, from the kitchen window, mom watches as another encounter with this bully plays out. Again, as things heated between me and him, I retreat to run back into the house. But this time, mom runs to the door and locked it! There I was, a locked door in front of me and a bully (who would like nothing better than to smash my brains out) behind me. I had no other place to go but into fight mode! As the story goes, it was a fast and furious attack... so much so that mom ran out of the house to pull me off the kid. He did not bother me again after this encounter.

It is worth noting retrospectively that mom's goal was not to promote or condone acts of violence, but to seize a teachable moment designed to instill courage and dignity in her son. That this came from a woman is not only equally noteworthy but stresses the point here. Women who are faithful, godly, morally decent human beings, are not only immeasurable partners in marriage, but critical guides and support for the home and humanity, to the extent that their absence dramatically affects family. As mentioned, there is significance to the adage, "as the family goes, so goes the community, and the church". Family has a significant impact on all other entities. The family is so significant to society, neither the church nor the government can ignore its health.[5, 6] The woman is key to a healthy family. This in no way suggests that the man is incapable of parenting effectively, whether in marriage or in singleness. It is, however, testament to the fact that God uniquely gifted the woman in these areas, it is a part of her being that profoundly contributes to our humanity. Some studies show that the absence of maternal care contributes to behavioral issues in children as they age.[7]

If these enter society less than optimal, it weakens society over-all, especially if we do not attend to these types of injuries.

Economy

Although well known by economist and other experts, many do not seriously entertain the staggering economic impact leveraged by any potential absence of the woman. While the woman frequently points to disadvantages in the workforce contributing to disproportionate wealth, experts do not make her economic relevance top priority or an important topic in conventional narratives. Expectations for this kind of conversation are less likely among those more interested in reducing her footprint. It is a banner they prefer not to hoist. The truth of the matter is that the woman wheels significant economic power, so much so, her absence will cause a major punch in the gut.

On March 8, 2017, International Women's Day, women around the globe staged a strike in the name of equal rights. They dubbed the event, A Day without A Woman.[8] The effort included women around the world taking that day off as a measured economic impact globally. The woman understands her economic value and sphere. For instance, per calculations produce by the Center for American Progress, according to the woman's salary and number of hours worked, woman power contributes 7.6 trillion to the nation's gross domestic product (GDP) annually, a total that is far north of Japan's GDP, 5.6 trillion.

The Center further notes that if the woman took off one day, it would cause a 21-billion-dollar impact.[9] In the McKinsey Global Institute's report titled, The Power of Parity, they showcase the woman's full economic power. Not only will advancing women's equality add 12 trillion to the global economy, if she "participates in the workforce identically to her male-counterpart, she will contribute 28 trillion to annual global GDP".[10] These are massive numbers that can produce significant impact on any society. She then is worthy of hire, recognition, and invitation to humanity's upward mobility.

Spiritual

Overzealous efforts to point out what she cannot do biblically often obscure the spiritual significance of the woman. Although I am not one to impugn holy scripture or veto divine adjudication,[11] I am convinced that the woman is far more critical to spiritual life than how many conventionally perceive her. Spiritual, in its fullest definition embodies the essence of God; the indwelling presence of the Holy Spirit, which is evident by the "fruit" He produces in the lives of those He dwells; among which are love, kindness, goodness, and gentleness, to name a few. In fact, because a Supreme Being created us with all these traits, some aspect of these is present in every human being. It then is not uncommon to find all these characteristics in a woman. As noted in chapter 6, the woman's predilection for God shows through her attendance and involvement in congregational life. In addition, are those good deeds or "good works" commonly associated with women in the community.

Because these acts of goodness are influential, impact from the absence of her is notable as well.

The woman usually unabashedly displays her faith; and proudly touts covenant relationship with the Lord, a fact especially common among African American women. But the woman's testimony herald through her benevolent work in the community and church is her greatest declaration of faith and spirituality. Testimony in this context, comes out of I Timothy 2:10, and from the Greek word (epangello) means to make a public announcement. The woman's acts of good works, kindness, love, and benevolence points to an abiding relationship with the Lord or reflect one created by God. The capacity for these in one's life not only honors God but blesses the community additionally. The broader context of the passage (I Timothy 2:9-15) not only signify the importance for the woman to align her good deeds with her testimony (epangello) but includes necessary attitude adjustments, supportive roles, and notable contributions to humanity, by raising and steering others into godliness.

Emphasis on the woman's spiritual significance is not a slight suggestion that hers is greater than the man. The Apostle Paul correctly notes the spiritual equality that exists between men and women before God.[12] Notwithstanding, we must not conflate this spiritual status with divinely inspired roles for men and women. The focus then is on the importance of her spirituality in critical contexts, and how her absence dramatically affects these. If her ontological and spiritual contributions were insignificant, there would be no adverse effects from her absence.

But that her spiritual contributions are important, adversity is likely in her absence. God calls the woman to be a teacher of things that are good,[13] both in her home and community. Her spiritual essence not only inspires, but it also informs. This cannot be more evident than in the home. Again, the emphasis is on the nucleus of society, the home. The Apostle Peter captures both the criticality and power of the woman's spiritual essence by noting that her behavior alone can turn her husband in the right direction, toward God.[14]

The woman's chaste and respectful behavior, coupled with the imperishable qualities of humility and a quiet strength, is precious in the sight of God. Her soft nature, born out of an abiding spiritual presence, has tentacles that extend deep into the heart of the home, church, and community. Removing the woman stifles progress, creates drudgery and will eventually lead to humanity's extinction. The madam then, is worthy of her place, and must take her seat; and lean into her God ordained role and power. She is one of the critical axes that turns humanity. If the madam is ever missing, the world will miss her treasure and contribution to life.

Who can deny that the Woman is worth celebrating?

The Promenade

A Dance in the Public Square

*I*n almost every society or community on the planet are women who have experienced challenges and difficulty simply because they are feminine. The vast reach of this dilemma reminds us of the haunting curse imposed by God on the human experience and is a tangible validation of the Genesis account. Even in the face of naysayers and doubters, the persistent clash between men and women affirms the details of the curse implemented thousands of years ago. The woman's life experience today certifies that throughout the annals of time men have predominantly held certain mental frameworks toward the woman; and women have held unique perceptions of life in the wake of the incessant fallout from her human experience.

While many covet better days in which we inoculated the woman from the horrid outcomes of maltreatment, the cycle continues globally. The unwanted truth of the matter is that there will be no end to this cycle. Because of divine adjudication, the clash between men and women will exist until the final consummation of all human affairs, the end of time. As indicated earlier, the ontology of men and women is such that the battle of the sexes is inevitably persistent. Notwithstanding, God has created a venue and medium through which humans can salvage and experience (to some extent) the peace and happiness once introduced in paradise lost.

But the process necessary to create such experiences must include divine mandates and ethical codes injected into humanity as a compass, not only navigating humanity into a covenant relationship with God, but the concourse leading us back to the other blessings of paradise. Among these mandates and codes are calls for the man to experience a fundamental change regarding the woman, for he must learn to see the woman through the eyes of the Creator; and the woman must learn how to filter her response to her environment through the heart of the Creator. Only then can she genuinely extend forgiveness to her male-counterpart. This chapter unpacks the critical mandate and ethical code necessary for humans (especially the woman) to reclaim the joys of paradise. Authentic change, genuine acts of forgiveness, reconciliation, and restoration will spawn dance that is both intricate and graceful, in celebration of the woman.

The Paradigm Shift

I detailed the undeniable and indispensable value of the woman in earlier chapters of this book. I will not revisit them entirely here, except to repeat that where I delineate her value, the aim is not to tell the woman she has value, for she knows this better than her male-counterpart.

Rather, the aim is (as a man) to state the obvious. It is a concession and acknowledgement of sorts... a significant change in which we see the woman solely through the eyes of the Creator. It is a view of the woman through divine motivation for creation. God's mandate regarding male and female noted in I Corinthians 11:7-12 encapsulates and highlights the point hoisted here. Although this passage contributes to women's grief all over the world, I invite you to shift from that emotion momentarily and embrace the richness of a truth seemingly hidden.

> For a man ought not to have his head covered, since he is the image and glory of God; but the woman is the glory of man. For man does not originate from woman, but woman from man; for indeed man was not created for the woman's sake, but woman for the man's sake. Therefore, the woman ought to have *a symbol of* authority on her head, because of the angels. However, in the Lord, neither is woman independent of man, nor is man independent of woman. For as the woman originates from the man, so also the man *has his birth* through the woman; and all things originate from God.
>
> NASB

I will resist temptation to produce a full exegesis of this passage, which (in truth) will broaden our understanding of it for life in the 21st century. Too often many read and digest this passage without knowledge and understanding the meaning in its original language, Korne Greek. Nevertheless, the point significant to our discussion here comes from verse nine, in which it states that "...the woman was created for the man's sake."[1] That God creates the woman for the man is undeniable.

We must process this as something more than a "Pauline" statement, and view this within the canon of Scripture. God does not give her or make her available to the man as a personal toy or commodity; she is a critical source and power necessary for completing a divine mission. The fact she originates from God for specific reasons, i.e., to assist man in the human experience, should not only occasion reverence for her as an ontological gift, but praise to God as Creator. As noted, "all things originate from God." It is a fact of which the woman too should remain mindful, and consistently present herself in every context. When men are mindful that God has given the woman as responsibility and help for his role in the human experience, many are less foolish and insensitive regarding interaction with the woman.

The Woman's Forgiveness

The second moral code is forgiveness, which is the "bedrock and hallmark" of the Christian faith; the linchpin that binds fallen man into a covenant relationship with his Creator. In chapter nine of volume one of the Phantom of Faith Series, I spend a significant amount of space detailing valuable components of forgiveness.[2] It is one moral ethic that challenges people's ability to practice authentically and effectively. Part of that difficulty develops out of an incomplete understanding of forgiveness as defined by God. I frame it this way because any of us can assign our own criteria and definition of forgiveness, but true forgiveness has divine principles embedded in it. The act of forgiveness is much more than accepting an apology or deciding not to enact some sort of retribution against another.

Forgiveness begins with self-analysis and includes divine precepts and consideration of the other. It not only partitions, pardon and dismisses fault, it restores rights and privileges;[3] and contributes to development of full personhood,[4] for the offender and the offended. We do not find the roots of forgiveness among men, but has its origin in God as an eternal attribute.[5] Where there is forgiveness, its immediate impact moves the offended into a divine space, in that there is no other act of righteousness or morality that makes us more like God than the act of forgiveness. Whenever we choose to forgive a transgression; an offense or injury, we become like the Creator at that moment. God's forgiveness of us should solely predicate the motivation to forgive others.[6] In this context the offender becomes a lesser issue, because the offense transfers out of the hands of the offender and offended into the hands of God. It then is not the man the woman sees, but rather, her God. It is her own sacrifice and concession of change.

Refusal to forgive has dire consequences eternally.[7] The premise for forgiveness then must be a genuine effort to be godlike and to do for others what God has done for you.[8] The measure or criteria usually employed to determine whether or when one should forgive a person depends heavily on the type of offense, who it affects, and the damage done. This, of course, is a human perspective and certainly not a process God uses. The other factor commonly used to determine or extend forgiveness is whether the person can provide restitution, the ability to right the wrong.

But what happens if such a person is incapable of correcting matters to your satisfaction. What if restitution is inadequate or sometimes completely out of reach? What if the injury from what they have done is so painful it protracts over a lifetime? Should you forgive? Many women emote and believe too many men have caused serious injury throughout time. But this prevailing context sets up an opportunity for the woman to become like the Lord. That there is no other point in which we are more like God than that moment we choose to forgive is apparent. But there is no greater opportunity, meaning and importance than that which is found in the act of forgiveness of someone who cannot make restitution; of one incapable of righting a wrong, or cannot pay the debt owed. Although monetary debt can fall into this discussion, it is not what is in mind here. This is a debt from moral injury. An injury so profoundly painful it brings a person's soul near the point of disintegration, a form of inexpressible suffering. When the woman extends forgiveness in this context, there is no other point in which she is more like the Lord. How, you ask?

When Jesus Christ died on the cross, He essentially paid debt you and I could never pay in full. The wage of sin is death.[9] He carried the weight and canceled the payment due. Note:

> ...having canceled out the certificate of debt consisting of decrees against us, which was hostile to us; and He has taken it out of the way, having nailed it to the cross.
>
> Colossians 2:14 NASB

We capture the beauty of forgiveness in more detail in the book of Leviticus chapter 16, in which it features the scapegoat as a prototype of Christ. What is significant is the Hebrew word for forgiveness, nasa, which has three semantic concepts that stress the true meaning of forgiveness. First is "to lift up" in the way one may lift a heavy object to rescue a person trapped beneath. The second is the idea bearing and carrying the sin away from the person and the community. This is what the scapegoat in Leviticus 16:21-22 captures. The process symbolically transferred the sins of the people to the goat and then sends it away from the guilty person and the community. It sends sin to a place where it can no longer live. Forgiveness takes the life out of sin. It has nowhere else to go afterwards. Choosing not to forgive allows the sin and error to live on. It gives it legs to continue to move through that environment, family, or community.

Third is the idea of "taking away sin" in contrast to carrying away. They are different. Taking away implies the removal of guilt, which in its fullness is the sole act of God. God, through Christ, removes guilt. It is justification.[10] After we extend forgiveness, we see and treat the one once guilty, as if the infraction never occurred. It is this aspect of forgiveness so many people fail, as persons and communities. People struggle to separate guilt from new opportunity. Continuing to see a person's guilt well after the fact, or better stated, beyond the point of forgiveness, nullifies any attempt to resolve the issue and restore the person to comradery. Satan uses this struggle to trap people in an unforgiving state, which immediately moves a person out of alignment with God into a position not safe for any of us to be.

But when we extend forgiveness, it paves the way for two other critical codes for moving into better relationship with God and peace with people in our environment, i.e., reconciliation and restoration. There is no way in which we realize true forgiveness independent of these. You cannot practice forgiveness authentically without reconciling and restoring.

Reconciliation

There are likely several other terms that come to mind when you hear reconciliation, i.e., compromise, settlement, or agreement. In psychological contexts, reconciliation is unrestricted openness, at least to self and other people with whom one it involves conflict and separation. Some see this process as an exchange between opposing parties, regarding narratives of events and unveil pain associated with it.[11] Reconciliation is not just a process and event, it is a decision typically born out of forgiveness. As noted, reconciliation that is real cannot happen without genuine forgiveness.

It requires looking inward as much as one looks out to the opposing party. It removes hostility and other phantoms aimed at thwarting resolution to injury and conflict. But the most beautiful depiction of reconciliation is that which is enacted by God in the redemption process. It suggests that the hostility that exists between man and God (because of sin) vacates because of the work of Christ; paying the penalty, canceling the debt owed. In fact, the Greek word for reconciliation in Romans 5:10 and II Corinthians 5:18-19 implies that God has "laid aside or withdrawn wrath."

Because of the work of Christ, He chooses not to do what He was going to initially, or if the penalty of sin is unmet. In similar ways, embracing reconciliation after we extend forgiveness moves the view of the other into a place of peace, tolerance, and causes one to step back from delivering a response that would only breed more conflict.

Restoration

It is a critical next step behind forgiveness and reconciliation. In some aspect, it is that part of forgiveness we must view as a component of the overall process. What is the point of forgiveness if it does not restore? What if God decides He will forgive us of our sins but send us to Hell, anyway? Fortunately, that would never be the case. People are not always good at restoration. This is largely because of a fixation on the wrong committed, which is a tale-tell sign that genuine forgiveness has not occurred. You cannot have forgiveness without restoration.

Our emotions can sometimes hinder the restoration process. However, in its most authentic form, forgiveness will move a person from the emotions generated by the initial issue or offense to critical thinking and spiritual discernment.[12] The word restore originates from the Greek word katartizo, which gives us a fuller view of its meaning. For instance, it means to repair something broken, like a bone; or to move pieces that are out-of-place back into place. Galatians 6:1-2 is a great exemplar of this, in that the word restore refers to restoring a Christian toppled by sin and error.

It implies placing something back into its former good condition, which is like popping a bone out of joint, back into its place. Until this happens, restoration has not taken place, and authentic forgiveness remains absent.

May I have this dance?

When the man shifts his perception and thought process regarding the woman, and sees her as a divine gift worthy of love and reverence, and protection; and cautiously interact with her in his fear of the Lord, he will begin the journey down the promenade celebrating the woman, and pose the question, may I have this dance? Dancing is an act of celebration. It promotes camaraderie, collaboration, and symphony. When the man and the woman learn to calibrate unity, they will promote God's agenda for humanity and glorify Him as Creator. The moment in which the woman elects to become like God by extending genuine forgiveness to her male-counterpart, reconciliation and restoration are inevitable.

But the efficacy of either approach is impalpable without embracing divine principles aimed at bringing all things into subjection and glory to God. The vibrant dance to the transcendent rhythm of holiness, kindness, love, joy, and peace will not only draw the man and the woman closer, but will bring a little of paradise to the public square.

The Ambience of Contextual Praise

Honoring God for Creating the Woman

*I*n the latter chapters of the Old Testament book of "Praises" (Psalm, 148-150, specifically) are calls to give homage and praise to God as Creator. The verses that are most notable among them are those in chapter 148 that praise the Lord because of His creative genius. The book closes with an exclamation for every created being to lift praise to God: "Let everything that has breath praise the Lord. Praise the Lord!" -Psalm 150:6. Given that He is Sovereign and Supreme, God's nature evokes praise, honor, and worship consistently. When the Lord was upon approach to Jerusalem, the crowd surrounding Him broke out into a loud praise. The Pharisees (a sect of Jews who opposes to Jesus) asked the Lord to silence the crowd. Instead, Jesus noted that if the people became silent, the rocks would cry out.[1] Signaling that as the Lord of Host, His creation will praise Him. Even within a human context, praise usually follows something good, unique, and successful. Children praise their virtuous mother;[2] and the community praises the work of the woman[3] or should, at least. If we can understand this in human contexts, how much more in spiritual contexts.

What is notably interesting about praise is that it is never silent. This is the message Jesus conveys to the Pharisees, who wanted to silence the crowd's praise of Jesus. Although the message that praise is not silent still rings true in contemporary times, there are churches and congregations whose ultra conservative read and approach to worship attempts to muffle the ambience of praise. The notion that religiosity and holiness hide in silence is misleading. Why would any saint want to temper a prodigious spirit percolating within? The word praise as noted in its original language refers to an exultation of sorts, jubilation. It is from where the word hallelujah derives.

Since praise is not silent, it is wise for us to understand its message exactly. For if praise is in fact not silent, it says something. Praise is more than a song and shout, or some feverish dance and celebration. There is order and intentionality embedded in the concept of praise. One aspect helping us understand the message behind praising is in the concept of praise as an act of worship. This explains why we should not seek praise from others and must be careful about how, who, and what we praise.[4] The highest praise men can have between them is praise that emanates from the Lord.[5]

The Hebrew and Aramaic words for praise reveal seven types of praise:
- Towdah- an act of thanksgiving, usually in songs of worship (Ps. 26:7; 42:4) and praise produced by a choir or during a procession (Nehemiah 12:31, 38)

- Shabach (pronounced, shaw-bakh) it means to address in a loud tone; triumph, glory and to commend someone; praise through words.
- Yadah- to hold out the hand to worship with extended hands; to give thanks, to confess or make confession.
- Barak- (pronounced, baw-rak) means to kneel, to bless as an act of adoration.
- Zamar (pronounced, zaw-mar) to celebrate in song and sing a psalm.
- Halal (pronounced, haw-lal) refers to celebration, to boast not of oneself necessarily, but of another.
- Tehillah (pronounced, tel-hil-law) acknowledging deeds worthy of praise; it points to the quality or attribute of a person or thing; a song that exalts God.

There is enough here for us to appreciate the fact praise has a message, it communicates and in effect is not silent. There is no one more worthy to be praised than the God of heaven, and for most people, that is understood. But for the sake of this writing, let us contextualize praise to highlight one aspect of praise to God we should vocalize in the public square. Context or "contextual" usually refers to the circumstances in which an event occurs; the setting from which something emanates.

As noted in chapter one, at some point prior to Genesis 1:1 the Trinity (God as Father, Son, and Holy Spirit) created and ordained a people in His likeness and image; for His pleasure and glory. There are only a few texts in Holy Scripture that give some insights of that conversation before time and space began.

One of which is noted John 17:5, 23. Without getting into the complexed doctrine of the Trinity, I suffice to say that God's agenda included the woman well before the earth forms. Chapter one highlights the fact when God is creating Eve (the first woman) in the Garden of Eden, He is working from a blueprint already formed before He created the universe. As I have stated repeatedly, this signals that the constituents or element of her ontology, God inspires. The good things that make the woman unique, and that gives her a soft grace that sweetens the human experience, have divine purpose. The woman reflects her Creator from the crown of her head to her inner being, her soul.

The contextual praise of which He is worthy has to do with the creation of the woman. From the wealth of His wisdom, He foraged a plan by which humans would come into being and ultimately realize His being, presence, and immense power, whether they believed and accepted Him. The woman was strategically instrumental to God's overarching agenda. God saturated the bible with extraordinary women, who have made substantial contributions to the human experience. But it was Mary whom God distinguishes for a task no other woman would ever experience, the human vessel through which the savior enters the world. A task ordained well before Mary was born and the New Testament period was vibrant. The woman is so significant to life, the world cannot survive without her. A created specialty placed in time and space as a conduit for love, wisdom, grace, and divinity. Who then is worthy of praise, except her maker?

The Ambience

What should be the voice and tenor of any praise offer to God in this context? That praise is not silent is indisputable. What then is the message of praise regarding the context of the woman's creation? The jubilant noise that should burst from humanity's heart should evince joy, thanksgiving and celebration for the woman's presence and impact on the human experience, obvious through these indelible contributions:

- Family: the woman's maternal gifts and presence are unmatched and has positively shaped the lives of people in her environment, whether biologically, blended or adopted.

- Community: her relentless care of the other binds the ties that forage healthy communities; her ongoing fight for justice, equality, and safety consistently creates consciousness of the need for reformation.

- Counsel: harnessing a unique wisdom, she has guided many out of threat and danger, into more productive spaces and contexts.

- Innovation: she has made her mark on the world as a competent contributor to business, education, medicine, and technology, to name a few; paving the way for those who follow; and shifting the narrative as fodder for better days ahead.

- Faith: her divinity shines bright, out numbering her male-counterpart in her devotion to God through the church and community; gifted with a unique ontology, she reflects her Creator through the love, grace, patience and sacrifice she gives to others.

There must be a noise of celebration in the public square regarding the woman, not only by the woman, but her male counterpart as well. Let him state the obvious too. The woman is a created specialty, valuable entity for the world. Although the woman is worthy of appreciation and reward for her tireless effort to be, become, and belong; and her impact on the world, it is God whom we must not forget to praise for this indispensable blessing to humanity. Made more beautiful than any other creature, she is the crowning jewel of the created order. We must celebrate the woman; and we must honor and praise God for her presence. Every time humanity extends equality and respect, we praise God; in each instance, we treat the woman with love and delicacy; we glorify God. The world honors the Lord when we use her gifts and talents appropriately. In every moment in which we protect her from harm spiritually and otherwise, we recognize her specialty. Every day is the "Day of the Woman." God's premeditated providential care of the world created an ineradicable gift to the world, WOMAN: Beauty Power and Divinity in Motion! Maybe she has been through the fire, but heat in the hands of a divine blacksmith produces an exceptional creation. When humanity sees the woman through the eyes of her Creator, He becomes the purpose for the ambience of praise.

Chapter One Notes & References

[1] www.wafflehouse.com/history/

[2] https//interactive.unwomen.org/womensfootprintinhistory

[3] I Timothy 6:15-16

[4] Exodus 17:14; I Kings 2:3, for example.

[5] The moment God the Father and Creator determined that He would create, everything was clearly defined (identity, purpose, scope, and timing etc..) by Him in that moment. God does not work "on-the-fly" but through His divine will, mission, and holiness. John chapter 17; Romans Ch. 8 and Ephesians help shed light on this biblical concept.

[6] Psalm 148:2, 5

[7] Matthew 22:30

[8] The First Law of Thermodynamics states that energy cannot be created or destroyed. See www.physicscentral.com for more information.

[9] Genesis 1:1-2:22

[10] www.space.com (January 10, 2017); www.ncbi.nlm.nih.gov (The Effect of Soil on Human Health: An Overview)

[11] Wilder Smith, A.E. (1987) The Scientific Alternative to Neo-Darwinian Evolutionary Theory; and Meyer C., Stephen (2009) Signature in the Cell

[12] Genesis 2:21

[13] Genesis 2:22

[14] Ibid Wider-Smith, Meyer

[15] Ibid

[16] A type of mistaken reasoning in which the form of an argument itself is invalid. McGraw-Hill (2012) Create pg. 133

[17] Gen. 2:22

[18] James 1:17

[19] Genesis 2:23

[20] Genesis 3:7

[21] I Timothy 6:7

[22] Gen. 2:23

[23] Gen. 1:27

Chapter Two Notes & References

1. The Liberty Illustrated Bible Dictionary (1986) Thomas Nelson Publishers, pg. 210
2. I Samuel 25:1-38
3. I Samuel 25:38
4. Romans 15:4
5. See: Meyer, Stephen C., (2009) Signature in the Cell DNA and The Evidence for Intelligent Design. Chapters 4 and 5
6. See Oxford Advanced Learner Dictionary (2008)
7. Kant, Immanuel (2010 ed) The Critique of Pure Reason. The original publication of work was made in 1781.
8. Bretherton I (1992). "The Origins of Attachment Theory: John Bowlby and Mary Ainsworth". Developmental Psychology. 28 (5): 759–775.
9. Christopher, H. (1876) The Remedial System. Transylvania Press, pg. 36

[1] For more information on this, see Sephanie Watson, The Unheard Female Voice. https://doi.org/10.1044/leader.FTR 1.24022019.44 Vocal Attributes. https://ww,v.britannica.com/topic/specch-lan guagc/voca 1-attri butcs

[2] There are those who believe God's mandate for the role and responsibility of the woman in the family and the church, is applicable in every sector and context. For example, these hold that a woman cannot become the president of a bank or a CEO of a corporation because it is a position of leadership. This is what I am calling "overreaching application". God is crystal clear regarding His expectation of the woman in the family, church, and society.

[3] Genesis 3:17

[4] Ibid v 17

[5] Ibid

[6] Zodiatcs, Spiros (1984) Hebrew/Greek Study Bible: Lexical Aids to the Old Testament. Pg. 1670; code 8085

[7] As cited in Britannica: Code-switching. Contributor: Carlos D. Morrison, Professor, Communications, Alabama Slale University al Montgomery. https:/jw,vw.hritannica.com/topic/code-sv,ritching

[8] Code Switching. https://www.hritannica.com/topic/code-switching

[9] https://www.merriam-wehster.cc,m/dictionary/seed

[10] Iowa Agriculture Literacy Foundation. https:/iowaagliteracy.word prcss.com/2018/05/04/scicncc-10 I-germination/

[11] The emotional space between individuals or groups and the measures used to determine such positions, attitudinal approach, and psychological fences.

[12] See: Ihdle, Don. (1976) Listening and Voice: A Phenomenology of Sound. Ohio University Press

[13] By environment, I mean the complex of social and cultural conditions affecting the nature of an individual community.

[14] Noah Salomon. What lies Beneath the Sands: Archeologies of Presence in Revolutionary Sudan. https://pomeps.org/what-lies-Beneath-the-sands-archaeologies-of-presence-in-revolutionary-sudan

15 National Geographic. November 2019. WOMEN: A Century of Change

16 Ibid. pg. 100

17 Dictionary of Mining, Mineral and Related Terms (pg. 921) U.S. Bureau of Mines 1968

18 See http://www.physicalgeography.net fundamentals/101.html for more information.

19 Geological Faults: Definition, Causes & Types. https://study.com/academy/lesson/geological-faults definition-causes-types.html

20 See http://www.physicalgeography.net/ fundamentals/101.html for more information.

Chapter Four Notes and References

1. See the Book of Esther, Chapter 4
2. Merriam Webster. https://merriam-webster.com/deictionary/mural
3. See Brizendine, Louann (2006) The Female Brian. Broadway Books
4. See: www.arts.gov/impact/creative-placemaking
5. www.insider.com/entertaiment
6. See: www.imdb.com/title/characters
7. See www.livescience.com
8. www.mirrorhistory.com
9. The New Testament Greek English Dictionary, Vol. 13. Pg. 276, no. 2627. The Complete Biblical Library
10. Thayer's Greek-English Lexicon of the New Testament (1977) pg. 334, code:2657. Baker Book House
11. Ibid, Vol. 15. Pg. 66, no. 3740. The Complete Biblical Library
12. Mussner, as cited in Cleon L. Rogers, Jr., and Cleon l. Rogers III (1998) The New Linguistic and Exegetical Key to the Greek New Testament. Zondervan Publishing House
13. Ibid Thayer, pg. 484
14. http://www.infiressources.ca

Chapter Five Notes & References

[1] Aesthetics concerns itself with the appreciation of beauty and good taste; it refers to a heighten sensitivity to beauty, guiding principles in matters of artistic beauty and taste; a branch of philosophy that deals with the origin of beauty. Philosophical and theological approaches to aesthetics points to the existence of God, and the best explanation for it. The Aesthetic Argument is founded on the concept that beauty speaks to an ordered universe, and its presence and purpose are determined by the Creator God. For quick references, see: https://www.oxfordhandbooks.com; Fran Burch, *Religious Aesthetics. A* Theological Study of Making and Meaning (London: Macmillan Press, 1990)

[2] See: Williams, Peter. Aesthetic Arguments for the Existence of God. Quodlibet Journal: Volume 3 Number 3, Summer 2001

[3] Genesis 1:1

[4] For additional information, see: https://smithsonianmag.com/science-nature/diamonds-unearthed-1416629226

[5] visible as alternating flashes of white and spectral-colored light and The contrast of dark and light that moves around the diamond.

[6] See https://www.discovermagazine.com/planet-earth/the-geology-of-rubies.

[7] Psalm 19:1

[8] Exodus 28:2

[9] Job 40:10; Psalm 27:4; 50:2

[10] I Chronicles 16:29; II Chronicles 20:21; Ps. 29:2

[11] Strauss, Mark S. (1979). "Abstraction of prototypical information by adults and 10-month-old infants". Journal of Experimental Psychology: Human Learning and Memory. American Psychological Association (APA). 5 (6): 618–632., and Kramer, Steve; Zebrowitz, Leslie; Giovanni, Jean Paul San; Sherak, Barbara (February 21, 2019). "Infants' Preferences for Attractiveness and Babyfaceness". Studies in Perception and Action III. Routledge. pp. 389–392.

[12] Isaiah 48:11; Daniel 4:35; Eph. 1:11

[13] Philippians 1:9. Before He commands His will, He declares it, i.e.,

in Exodus 20: 1-ff, He declares or make known the Ten Command-
ments by which men should live. He will always tell us what do,
before demanding we do it.

14 Philippians 2:13

15 Psalm 11:7; Matthew 5:48; I Peter 1:16

16 One of the most famous biblical narratives that illustrate this truth
is found in Exodus chapter 3, which chronicles Moses' initial en
counter with the Holy One. As Moses turns to approach God, He
calls out for him to remove his shoes in honor and respect of his
holiness. Although the presence of God is truncated, had He not
called out to him, Moses would have stepped into His
presence unprepared, the results of which would have been death.
The significance of God's holiness is emphasized when Moses re
Quested permission to see God face-to-face, to behold His glory, to
which the Holy One replies: "You cannot see My face, for no man
can see Me and live." Exodus 33:17-22

17 Ecclesiastes 3:11

18 Beauty | Definition of Beauty by Oxford Dictionary

19 Lexical Aids to the Old Testament. Key Word Study Bible: 2895,
2896. AMG Publishers

20 See Hebrew and Aramac Dictionary in Strong's Exhaustive Con
cordance of The Bible. Red Letter Edition. Thomas Nelson

21 Stanford Encyclopedia of Philosophy 1999

22 Online Etymology Dictionary for additional information: ety
monline.com

23 See dictionary.com/beauty

24 Gorodeisky, Keren (2019). On Liking Aesthetic Value. Philosophy
and Phenomenological Research.

25 Hoderich, Ted (2005). "Beauty". The Oxford Companion to
Philosophy. Oxford University

26 The dimensionless ratio of the circumference of the waist to
the hips. This is calculated as waist measurement divided by hip
measurement ($^W/_H$).

27 Waist Circumference and Waist-Hip- Ratio, Report of a WHO
Expert Consultation (PDF). World Health Organization. 8-11

28 For more information, see: DoCarmo, Stephen. Notes on the "Black
Cultural Movement".

29 Begley, Sharon (2009). The Link Between Beauty and Grades.
Newsweek

30 Amina A Memon; Aldert Vrij; Ray Bull (2003). Psychology and
Law: Truthfulness, Accuracy and Credibility. John Wiley & Sons.

31 Lorenz, K. (2005). Do Pretty People Make More. CNN, Time
Warner Cable News Network

32 See: Leo Gough (June 29, 2011). C. Northcote Parkinson's
Parkinson's Law: A modern-day interpretation of a management
classic. Infinite Ideas. p. 36.

[33] Acts 10:34-35; James 2;1-9

[34] John 1:18

[35] John 4:24

[36] I Timothy 1:17; 6:15-16; Colossians 1:15

[37] In those few instances in the bible where humans appear to have direct interaction with God (Theophany) are moments in which God adjusts himself to appear before them, i.e., Adam and Eve (Gen. chapters 2 and 3). Moses' encounter with God is intriguing. Not just his initial encounter at the burning bush (Ex. 3:1-6) but the more intimate encounter that emerges after he develops a more meaningful relation with God. He communes with the Creator "face -to- face" (Exodus 33:11). But even in this case, careful analysis of the text show that God appears in the cloud to commune and speak with Moses, which suggests that even in this context he is buffered from full exposure to the face of the almighty. The phrase "face-to-face" captures the intimacy of their relationship.

[38] Ibid SEE NOTE 37

[39] I Timothy 6:16

[40] Exodus 3:2

[41] Acts 9:1-9

[42] John 1:1, 14, 18; 14: 9-11; 17:5, 8, 11, 21-22; II Cor. 5:19

[43] Hebrews 1:3

[44] John 14:9

[45] Taylor, E. Joan (2018) What Did Jesus Look Like. Bloomsbury T&T Clark Publishing

[46] Balthasas von, Urs Hans (2009) The Glory of the Lord: A Theological Aesthetics 2nd Edition. Ignatius Press, San Fransico, pg. 58

[47] There are theologians who disagree over the division between spirit and soul. Their position is that it is always used interchangeably, but never separate. Irrespective of the debate, one thing is certain, man is at least, a dual Being, part material (body) and part immaterial (spirit). Another way of viewing this perhaps, is to understand what happens at after death. The body will return to the dust, the spirit goes back to God, and then there is the soul, which lives eternally, either in heaven or hell.

[48] www.toyota.com/jp

[49] Job 38:7. The words "morning stars" and "sons of God" is language that refers to the angelic realm, God's ministering spirits.

[50] Psalm 148:2, 5; Col. 1:16. Angles were created by fiat, which means God spoke them into existence. They are literally God-breathed.

[51] Genesis 1:1

[52] Zodhiates, Spiros 1991 Lexical Aids to the Old Testament (1254) in The Hebrew-Greek Study Bible pg. 1604

[53] See www.medicine.net

[54] What Makes Something Beautiful? | A Christian Guide to Beauty

and Design Part 4. Retrieved from: htpp//: thebibleisart.com

[55] Parker, H. Dewitt. The Principles of Aesthetics. Ch. 5: The Analysis of the Aesthetics Experience: The Structure of Experience

[56] See I Corinthians 12:11-26

[57] The Indian Journal of Endocrinology and Metabolism 2011 Sep; 15(Suppl3): S156–S161. doi: 10.4103/2230-8210.84851 The Orgasmic History of Oxytocin: Love, Lust, and Labor

[58] Isaiah 43:7; Revelation 4:11

[59] Matthew 11:28-30

[60] Hebrews 1:14

[61] See Grudem, Wayne (2020) Systematic Theology 2nd Ed. Zondervan Academic

[62] Ibid

Chapter Six Notes and References

[1] See www.meriam-webster.com

[2] John 6:37

[3] See Matt. 25:34; John chapter 17; specifically verses 6-10; 24

[4] Deuteronomy 7:6-8; Eph. 5:27; I Peter 2:9

[5] Isaiah 43:7; Revelation 4:11

[6] Gallup Jr., George H. Dec. 17, 2002 Why Are Women More Religious?

[7] See: U.S. Religious Landscape Study (2014) Retrieved from https//pewresearch.org

[8] Ibid

[9] The Gender Gap in Religion Around the World (March 22, 2016) Pew Research Center. https://pewresearch.org

[10] Stark, Rodney. 2002. Physiology and Faith: Addressing the Universal Gender Difference in Religious Commitment. Journal for the Scientific Study of Religion.

[11] Miller, Alan S., and John P. Hoffmann. 1995. Risk and Religion: An Explanation of Gender Differences in Religiosity.

[12] Bradshaw, Matt, and Christopher G. Ellison. 2009. The Nature-Nutrue Debate is Over, and Both Sides Lost! Implications for Understanding Gender Differences in Religiosity. Journal for the Scientific Study of Religion.

[13] Ibid

[14] In sociological contexts, secularization is the transformation of a society from close identification with religious values and institutions toward nonreligious values and secular institutions.

[15] Trzebiatowska, Marta, and Steve Bruce. 2012. "Why Are Women More Religious Than Men?" Pages 172-175

[16] De Vaus, David, and Ian McAllister. 1987. Gender Differences in Religion: A Test of the Structural Location Theory

[17] Schnabel, Landon. The Gender Pray Gap: Wage Labor and the Religiosity of High-Earning Women and Men

[18] Matthew 1:18-25

[19] See: Is Maternal Instincts Only for Moms? Here is the Science. May 9, 2018. National Georgraphic.com

[20] Ibid

[21] I John 4:7-21

[22] See: Proverbs 10:12; I Corinthians 13:1-13; I Peter 4:8

Chapter Seven Notes and References

1. See Phantoms of Faith Vol. I, Hidden Challenges of Faith and How to Navigate Them. Chapter 11, pgs 433-434
2. Matthew 16:17-18
3. Weust S., Kenneth (1973) Weust's Word Studies from the Greek New Testament. Vol. III, pg. 48
4. Revelation 14:13
5. Eph. 2:2; 6:12
6. Revelation 20:1-2
7. Revelation 12:12
8. II Corinthians 4:4; Galatians 4:8
9. Genesis 6:1-5. There have been much debate surrounding this passage. Here, "sons of God" is or can be translated to mean angels. There are various names for angels in Scripture. It is believed this was Satan's attempt to contaminate the pure line leading to the birth of Christ.
10. Wayne Grude is distinguished research professor of theology and biblical studies at Phoenix Seminary in Phoenix, Arizona; and author of Systematic Theology among several other publications.
11. Genesis 3:16
12. A life of holiness, love, forgiveness; respect for divine order and systems implemented to produce happiness and harmony between people, are just a few essentials for restoring the relationship God always intended for people to have and experience.
13. Zodhiates, Spiros Lexical Aids to the Old Testament in King James Hebrew and Greek Study Bible. Pg. 1,677; #8669
14. Ibid, pg. 1598 #376
15. See https://boatinternational.com/luxury
16. Zodhiates, Spiros. Lexical Aids to the New Testament in King James Hebrew and Greek Study Bible

Chapter Eight Notes and Referenecs

1. Humphreys, M. Jeffery. (2018) The Multicultural Economy. Selig Center for Economic Growth, University of Georgia.
2. There are multiple definitions for the term. However, for the purposes of this writing or chapter, madam refers to a form of polite address of the woman, the wife, mother grandmother, or woman of the house etc.
3. Families in a Changing World: Progress of the World's Women 2019-2020. Un Women. https://www.unwomen.org/en/digital-library/progress-of-the-worlds-women
4. Genesis 3:20
5. See: Feminine Perspectives on Reproduction and the Family. October 21, 2013. Stanford Encyclopedia of Philosophy. Retrieved https://plato.stanford.edu
6. Deuteronomy 6:4-7
7. Jay Belsky, Deborah Lowe Vandell, Margaret Burchinal, K. Alison Clarke-Stewart, Kathleen McCartney, Margaret Tresch Owen, The NICHD Early Child Care Research Network (2007) Are There Long-Term Effects of Early Child Care? Child Development 78 (2), 681-701.
8. A Day Without a Woman (2017) Center for American Progress. https:/americanprogress.org
9. Ibid
10. The Power of Parity: How Advancing Women's Equality Can Add 12 Trillion To Global Growth. (2015) Mckinsey Global Institute httpp://Mckinsey.com/mgi
11. Genesis 3:16
12. Galatians 3:28
13. Titus 2:3
14. I Peter 3:1-4

Chapter Nine Notes and References

[1] Genesis 2:18-23

[2] Hidden Challenges of People of Faith and How to Navigate Them. (2019) Vol. One, Phantoms of Faith. Pgs. 301-325

[3] Ibid

[4] The capacity for attributes like morality, consciousness and reason; critical elements constituting wholeness of a person of which fellow ship with God is essential.

[5] Exodus 34:7; Nehemiah 9:17; Daniel 9:9

[6] Eph. 4:32

[7] Matthew 6:15

[8] Matthew 6:12

[9] Genesis 2:17; Romans 6:23

[10] Romans 5:1-2

[11] Howes, Ryan. Forgiveness vs. Reconciliation. Forgiveness: Fact or Fiction https://psychologytoday.com

[12] Ibid, pg. 316

Chapter Ten Notes and References

1. Luke 19:40
2. Proverbs 31:28
3. Proverbs 31:38
4. Proverbs 27:21; Matthew 6:1-5
5. Matthew 25:21; I Corinthians 4:5

Phantoms of Faith Series
Volume III

THE
BLACKSMITH

...g the invisible hand in the heat
...fires of life.

E. D. ALLEN

COMING SOON!

E. D. ALLEN, D MIN. PHD.

Minister Emeritus | Theologian

PERFECTING THE CALL

"In the wake of the incessant pursuit for meaning and identity amid inevitable paradoxes and struggles spawned by the human experience, I realize life's most pressing duty is to obey God and perfect one's calling and election."

Dr. Allen has decades of experience in ministry. In addition, his professional experience includes mental health, forensic psychology consultancy, a court declaration as an Expert Witness in three areas of behavioral health, practice as a Child and Family Investigator (CFI) former CEO for humanitarian nonprofit organizations.

His tenure in ministry, specialized mental health, and executive leadership creates a unique perception and approach to contemporary challenges facing the church and community in the 21st century.

CPSIA information can be obtained
at www.ICGtesting.com
Printed in the USA
BVHW010054050821
613618BV00020B/97

9 780578 942179